# Crafting with
# Flea Market Fabrics

# Crafting with
# Flea Market Fabrics

Deborah Harding

Reader's Digest

The Reader's Digest Association, Inc.
Pleasantville, New York/Montreal

# Crafting with Flea Market Fabrics

A Reader's Digest Book

**Art Director**
Jean Locke Oberholtzer

**Directions Editor**
Eleanor Levie

**Photographer**
Geoffrey Gross

**Pattern Illustrations**
Phoebe Adams Gaughan
Ruth Schmuff

Library of Congress Cataloging in Publication Data

Harding, Deborah
    Crafting with flea market fabrics/Deborah Harding.
    p.   cm.
    Includes bibliographical references and index.
    ISBN 0-7621-0023-0
    1. Textile crafts.   2. Household linens—Recycling.
    3. Flea markets.   I. Title.
TT699.H37   1998                        97-31112
746—dc21

I gratefully dedicate this book
to my friend and colleague
Rosemary Drysdale,
who, patiently and generously,
crafted many of the projects that appear in this book,
and
to the memory of my mother,
Anita Hutchinson Harding.
Perhaps just a little of her ingenuity rubbed off on me after all.

# *Contents*

## 5 Handkerchiefs 80

## 6 Kitchen Linens 98

## 7 Doilies 114

## 8 General Directions 130

Working With Embroidered Linens, Chenille,
Quilts, Lace Trims & Doilies, Handkerchiefs,
and Kitchen Linens **132**

# *Introduction*

If you're at all like me, you not only "brake for yard sales," as the bumper sticker says, but chances are you make a habit of surfing flea markets on weekends and seldom pass up a tempting tag sale or thrift shop.

Flea-marketing is one of the fastest growing leisure-time activities after gardening—and you don't even have to get your hands dirty!

Most of us enjoy these relaxed shopping excursions in the company of a friend, spouse, or other relative. We collect several different things, buy collectibles as gifts, prefer to spend under $25 per item (under $10 is better yet), and frequently make impulse buys based on happy nostalgia.

Many sociologists think that as Baby Boomers approach the new millennium, we are clinging to kinder, gentler, and seemingly emotionally secure memories of childhood: the days when an evening of family entertainment meant gathering around the TV set with a bowl of popcorn on Sunday night to watch *The Ed Sullivan Show,* and "collectibles" usually referred to baseball cards.

For example, how often have you overheard someone at a country flea market reminisce fondly, "My mother served Sunday dinner on dishes like these"; or, "I remember one of those tablecloths in my grandmother's kitchen," followed hastily by, "Let's find out how much she'll take for it"; or, "Look at the handwork in those doilies, what a shame that people don't use them anymore!"

These are just some of the not-so-subliminal messages that contribute to the pleasure of the casual collecting experience.

In home decorating, tradition and "timeworn" are trendy. Hand-me-downs and handmade are in. Pieces of our heritage are welcome parts of the present. A sense of history (yes, the 1950s and even the 1960s now qualify as "history") is combined with whimsy and originality. Matching sets of dining room chairs, dishes, and linens have been replaced by mix-and-match.

However, there's more to collecting than the thrill of the hunt—the real challenge is what to do with your bounty after you get it home.

If you have bureau drawers or attic trunks overflowing with assorted too-good-to-pass-up linens, and laces, less-than-perfect chenille bedspreads, and throwaway quilts, this book is just what you've been waiting for. It's also a license to buy all those things you love but hesitate to, asking yourself, "Do I really need this?" Now you do.

This book is a fun—but practical—guide on how to shop and sew and cut and glue to transform your purchases and packed-away possessions into decorating accessories, toys, ornaments, and gifts.

Each of the first seven chapters concentrates on a different category of collectibles and provides you with bargain-hunting hints, price guidelines, and numerous ideas for creating your own designs. An array of projects, accompanied by easy-to-follow directions, require little or no experience and can be completed in a weekend—or even a single afternoon.

It won't take a magic wand or cyberspace technology to transform an embroidered table runner into a window panel or to underscore the shelves of a rustic armoire with crocheted lace edgings (once hand-stitched to trim linen sheet sets—before the no-iron variety). Embroidered guest towels, Valentine handkerchiefs, and crocheted doilies are just a few of the flea-market buys that are perfect for pillows tops. Quilt remnants and kitchen tablecloths can turn into Christmas stockings and teddy bears. A chenille bedspread is ideal for a shower curtain or a settee cushion.

By no means am I suggesting cutting up priceless antiques or pricey fabrics. What we're talking about are innovative ways to rescue and recycle vintage household linens that are slightly damaged—or simply discarded—and to give them new life.

Working with these textiles is very rewarding. Aside from the satisfaction of finding a bargain and then the feeling of accomplishment when you've

transformed it into your own heirloom, you establish a link with the past. When you admire the doily pillows you've made for your bed, pause just long enough to imagine the woman who created them: Were they made to go into her hope chest, were they a gift from mother to daughter, were they displayed on the furniture in someone's front parlor? Or was the mended holiday tablecloth that you have turned into a tote used to celebrate a family's Christmas year after year? Think what a pleasure it would be for the person who embroidered a 1940s pillowcase to know that even though it did wear out in places, it's now an adorable doll that delights a five-year-old.

Chapter Eight, General Directions, reviews basic sewing and crafting techniques and also provides helpful hints for laundering and working with vintage textiles.

Some people should probably be advised to proceed with caution. Crafting with flea market fabrics can become habit-forming. It's hard to pass up anything with potential and not think to yourself *I wonder what I could make with that*. You'll find yourself inspired to collect all kinds of additional treasures you never even considered before and, of course, you'll just *need* to find more time to shop!

Deborah Harding

Pillowcases are the perfect choice for dressing these adorable dolls. Originally known as "Homestead" or "Depression" dolls, they're favorites with children of all ages.

# Chapter One

# Embroidered Linens

Tea towels, dresser scarves,
and pillowcases are just
some of the many household
linens that our grandmothers
decorated with hand
embroidery. Made in great
quantities, from commercial
patterns, these flea-market
bargains are readily available
and present all kinds of
options for creative new uses.

The phrase "A Woman's Work Is Never Done" is put to rest with this bedroom set made up of days-of-the-week towels. For the bedspread, embroidered sections are appliquéd onto yellow dish towels, which are then stitched together.

*R*emember when your mother used to say "don't use the good towels, they're for the company?" Well, chances are that she was talking about the hand-embroidered guest towels that were proudly displayed in the powder room when friends came to visit. As luck would have it, few guests had the audacity to use them either, and, for that reason, there is an abundance of them available—in good condition—at flea markets these days.

### A LITTLE HISTORY

In the first half of this century, embroidery patterns were available from thread and other sewing supply manufacturers at little or no charge. Ads and offers appeared regularly in numerous women's magazines and newspaper sections. Women could choose not only the design but also the type of pattern to order and prices varied.

Designs pre-stamped on fabric were the most costly. For example, a 1912 issue of *McCall's* advertised a violet-pattern luncheon set consisting of a centerpiece and six doilies *stamped on fabric* for 65 cents (or given free for two magazine subscriptions). The same violet design was available for only 15 cents as a perforated pattern "for those who wish to use their own goods." A *perforated pattern* was one with tiny holes in it: The pattern was applied to the fabric by rubbing it with a blue chalky substance that penetrated the holes. To create your own perforated pattern, wheels with pointed edges could be purchased. The wheel rolled over a design to make pin pricks. Another option was a *transfer pattern,* which was printed on thin tissuelike paper and could be traced onto fabric with carbon paper or used with the wheel. Sometimes, you will come across embroideries that still have the paper attached: In this instance, someone simply pinned or basted the tissue pattern to the fabric and then stitched over it, intending to tear the paper away when finished. Later on, *iron-on patterns* gained in popularity, and, by 1961, *The Workbasket* magazine featured an entire section of designs that could be removed directly from the magazine and "used more than once before the iron cooled down."

**Morning, noon, and nighttime too, these oversized tea-towel pillows are perfect for relaxing in a porch swing or watching old movies on TV. A red border stripe woven into the original towel was cut and saved to frame the appliquéd message.**

Access to photocopiers, for enlarging and reducing patterns, was not available. Therefore, a woman who wanted blue birds (a symbol of luck and happiness) on her pillowcases and maybe on her hand towels as well needed to purchase several different-size patterns. That explains why the July 1916 issue of *Home Needlework Magazine* advertised blue bird patterns from several different companies: Collingbourne Mills in Elgin, Illinois, offered a "Pillow Top FREE" with four blue birds stamped on fabric along with the words "May Happiness Be Yours." It came in a package with instructions, a diagram, and two skeins of floss for only 10 cents in postage. As if that was not enough, in the same issue, Richardson Silk Company of Chicago offered a "Blue Bird Pin Cushion Outfit," which came complete with one blue bird stamped on linen, two skeins of Richardson's silk embroidery floss, R. M. C.

Cordonnet Cotton for a crocheted edging, and a "Sure Guide Embroidery & Crochet Lesson" all for 25 cents including postage.

Stylized basket designs with fruit and flowers, kitchen scenes, and even blue birds began to wane in popularity by the 1960s. In vogue were toadstools and mushrooms, fish, long-stem flowers, and peacocks. Prices had kept up with inflation and a complete kit for a pair of pre-stamped Birds of Paradise pillow tops was $5 from Bamberger's in New Jersey.

Over the years, these mass-market designs were ordered, and embroidered, by thousands of stitchers. This is why we see the same motifs appearing over and over again (in different variations and color preferences) on towels, dresser scarves, napkins, pillowcases, and other household linens. For shoppers, and inventive crafters, these hand-embroideries are treasures waiting to be found.

### TEA TOWELS

Towels alone offer all kinds of quick-change possibilities. Guest towels, which are also referred to as hand towels, are frequently embellished with flowers (often in a basket), birds, borders, sayings, or any combination of these elements. Towels intended for kitchen use—dish towels—are often embroidered with words and designs announcing their intended use, such as "Glassware," "China," or "Silver."

Not as plentiful, but certainly available, are days-of-the-week towels, which spelled out a woman's chores: "Monday for Laundry," "Tuesday for Ironing," "Wednesday for Mending," etc. Some days-of-the-week kitchen towels originated from feed sacks: Companies even provided the pattern already printed on them. A feed bag measured 38 inches (96.5cm) x 18 inches (46cm); if you find the larger-size towels, this is probably their history. On most days-of-the-week towels, you'll find the figure of a woman hard at work with the tools of the trade. Three little kittens were shown doing chores in the 1950s as well as hoop-skirted women with bonnets and parasols who managed to clean, bake, and wash with a playful puppy at their heels, and, by the 1960s, "Wilbur the Calf" made a brief appearance.

**Just one dresser scarf is all it took to make up both this fanciful cat and teddy bear. Notice how the embroidered flowers from one end of the scarf form the face of the teddy bear and the flowers from the other end are used on the body of the cat.**

Silk-embroidered, self-fringed linens were used to design this exquisite christening gown. The violet pattern was popular in the first quarter of the 20th century. Coasters make up the sleeves, bodice, and hem border. The front is fashioned from a matching centerpiece cloth.

Pick a bunch of flower-motif guest towels and make them up into an arrangement of wraparound pillow covers. Tie the sides with bows of pin-dot grosgrain ribbon.

### SHOPPING FOR TOWELS

When deciding which towels to buy, it helps to have a specific project in mind. Think about the size and condition you'll need. For example, if you want to make a set of pillows with a theme, you may want to concentrate on all floral stitcheries and/or on a specific color scheme.

If you intend to make a pillow, it's important that the entire embroidered section be in good condition and, as pillows are often handled, the backs need to be in decent condition as well. Consider whether a hem-stitched, colored border is an asset or a distraction. If you're making six pillows, just one colored border might be a distraction, but if you deliberately choose several colored borders, then it can be an eye-catching effect. If both ends of the towel happen to be decorated (note our scalloped one), you'll want to wrap it around the pillow to showcase both ends

My favorite finds are towels with words. Look for "Forget Me Not" or "Remember Me" for a neighbor who's moving away; "Sweet Dreams" for a child, "Home Sweet Home" for a new homeowner, or "Keep Smiling" for a friend who's going through a transition.

Most of the towels shown here have been purchased for $3 to $12, depending on their condition and the amount of embroidery. Towels with unusual sayings are the more expensive ones. Many people refer to this whole category of linen towels as tea towels.

If you find a complete, pristine set of seven days-of-the-week towels (possibly made for a hope chest or received as a gift and never used), you may simply want to frame them or use them for the purpose for which they were originally intended. A set of the "Three Little Kittens," in good condition, can be priced at $50 to $75 and a set with African-American figures can be as high as $150. For the projects in this chapter, I was shopping with recycling in mind and looking for imperfect towels: I bought one set of the larger size for $20. Stitched on different fabrics, some were much more worn than others. These towels were interesting because each had a hand-embroidered edging on all sides. They were a challenge to work with as the pictorial embroidery was positioned in the corners and on a diagonal. The set of more traditionally sized cross-stitch days-of-the-week towels cost $28. Some of these had permanent, discolored crease lines that couldn't be laundered out (the dealer had tried). A combination of all the towels was used in our bedspread set; the ones in better condition as shams or a pillow and the less perfect ones cut and appliquéd onto the spread.

There's no need to buy only sets; an assortment of these daily towels is fun to collect and can result in interesting projects. Individual ones also have their advantages and are usually priced between $4 and $10. A "Sunday" towel made into a pillow might

This guest towel seemed to lend itself to the cover of a guest book. It could also have developed into a mini-pillow to hang on the knob of a guest-room door.

An embroidered dresser (or vanity) scarf is the ideal solution for a narrow window treatment. All this one needed was a simple casing, top and bottom, to hold curtain rods.

The border of a worn kitchen towel was perfect for getting the message across on an eyeglass case. Sometimes a single word or an initial will inspire a project.

For conversation-piece place mats, collect kitchen towels with lettering along the bottom of one edge and add a layer of light padding to the part that rests on the table. One was adapted for a chair-back cover.

be a great gift idea for a church friend or one with a baking motif can be transformed into an apron for someone who loves to cook.

Dish towels have a little more wear-and-tear than guest towels as they are used on a daily basis. But don't be discouraged if there are spots or holes. I found a towel with the word "Glasses" stitched on it for only $2. It had not been sold because it had a large hole at one end and a bad rust stain. However, the embroidered part was perfectly salvageable and it was made up into the eyeglass case that you see here. A "Tea Towel" for $6 (not too many people serve formal tea these days) cried out to

be made into a tea cozy. Although towels are a good place to start, there are endless other possibilities to explore when thinking about new uses for old linens.

### DRESSER SCARVES

Embroidered dresser scarves are especially desirable because of their generous size. Often made in sets to fit the pieces of furniture in a bedroom (bureaus, vanities, chests, washstands, and bedside tables), they come in a variety of sizes. Usually, they average 14 inches (35.5cm) to 18 inches (46cm) in width and 40 inches (101.5cm) to 45 inches (114.5cm) in length but there are many exceptions as you'll soon discover. "Buffet scarves," used on a folded side table or dessert cart, are smaller than table runners but larger than bureau scarves. They are a practical size for sewing projects. All of these scarves are embroidered only at the ends. The middle is plain, as this part was covered when in use. Whatever your need, there's probably an embroidered scarf to fit the project if you keep your eyes open and your tape measure handy.

I bought one dresser scarf for $3 (it had some small snags in it) and, because of the amount of fabric to work with, made it into two toys (the teddy bear and the cat). Another day I found one to fit a window panel—in excellent condition—for only $6 and simply added a casing at the top and the bottom to make it into a curtain treatment.

### PILLOWCASES

Also plentiful and desirable are embroidered pillowcases. Matching pairs with well-executed embroidery and a crocheted or tatted edging usually start at $25 to $35. Individual cases average $8 to $15. You will see simpler designs with little or no edging for less money and ones with deep intricate edgings for more. Worn spots and any discoloration are likely to show up near the center, which is the section that was actually used to sleep on. Lavish, special-occasion pillowcases that were seldom used may have crease marks from folds. Therefore, it's a good idea to fully open a pillowcase (even though it's in a plastic bag) and

Even if you don't plan formal tea parties very
often, this tea towel turned into a tea cozy can be
enjoyed any time at all. To make it reversible,
choose a different towel for each side.

This $3 crib sheet, with a pink, hem-stitched border and the word "Baby" embroidered in pastels, seemed destined to be a curtain in a nursery. Floral-patterned ribbon was added to the bottom edge.

examine its condition before you buy it. Some of the most popular motifs are colonial ladies, flowers of all varieties, blue birds, swans, butterflies, children (usually girls), bows, and border treatments.

If the edging goes all around—and it almost always does—pillowcases make appealing skirts or sundresses for toddler-age girls. They are also charming as seat cushions (imagine three or four, in a row, on a window seat) and can fit over a ladder-back chair with just a little alteration. Opened at the seams, pillow-cases can be used as café curtains or made into sink or vanity skirts. I bought two different pillowcases and used them to dress a pair of traditional-style "Depression" or "Homestead" muslin dolls.

### TIPS TO REMEMBER

Naturally, how you plan to use your linens will influence your shopping choices but always keep an open mind. You never know what might attract your attention and spark your imagi-nation. These household linens are practical for many uses, as they were made to be laundered.

Don't overlook monograms embroidered on napkins, towels, and pillowcases. If your name is "Stern," you might want to col-lect "S" monograms in different styles, but all white-on-white, and then group them together as pillows. Initials can also be used to spell out a message either with pillows or on a quilt top. For a bride-to-be, friends might each shop for a different monogrammed towel and then join them all together for a quilt or tablecloth. Look for ones that say "Mr." and "Mrs." and place them in the center of your design.

"His" and "Hers" towels and pillowcases are often passed by at thrift shops and flea markets as being dated. Consider, how-ever, getting one towel that says "Hers" and transforming it into a baby bib, or try a couple as pockets on a little girl's pinafore. Collect eight or ten "His" and stitch them together for a baby coverlet.

At a time when we're used to no-iron fabrics, these hand-made linens are not appreciated by all shoppers. Therefore, if you're lucky, you may find a dealer who has just bought out an entire linen closet at an estate sale and will give you a special price if you buy a large quantity.

It's doubtful that you'll ever be able to look at these once taken-for-granted embroidered linens again without at least pausing for a minute and thinking "I wonder how that would look as a . . ."

**Sugar and spice and everything nice is conveyed by this doily appliquéd to a feeding bib for a youngster. It would also be charming on the bodice of a child's dress.**

**A chance encounter with a single linen napkin stitched with the words "Sweets to the Sweet" inspired this enchanting bib for an infant. The words "His" or "Hers" from a towel or pillowcase could also be used.**

# Pillowcase Dolls

**Size:** 20 inches (51cm) tall

## What You'll Need for Each Doll

▶ ⅝ yard (.6m) muslin fabric, for doll body
▶ Embroidered pillowcase (these have crocheted edgings)
▶ Pearl cotton embroidery thread or fabric marking pens, for face and hair
▶ Ribbon: 1½ yards (1.4m) satin, ⅜ inch (1cm) wide; and scrap of narrow green grosgrain ribbon
▶ Sewing thread to match fabrics and ribbon
▶ Polyester fiberfill for stuffing
▶ Small (baby) snap, for back of dress
▶ 57 large seed beads, ⅛ inch (3mm)
▶ Sewing, embroidery, and beading needles

## What To Do

1 Enlarge the patterns to full size and cut out. Fold muslin lengthwise in half and arrange pattern pieces for the doll on top, with long dash lines along the fold. Cut out 2 head/body pieces, for front and back, and 4 leg pieces.

2 For the face and hair, embroider as shown in photo, using French knots for eyes and hair and straight stitches for a nose and smile, or draw with fabric marking pens.

3 Place doll pieces together in matching pairs, with right sides facing. Sew ¼ inch (6mm) from edges; leave body and legs unstitched between O marks. Clip into the seam allowances as indicated on patterns, and turn pieces to right side. Stuff firmly with fiberfill. For legs, stuff to knee joints, pinch the sides in, and stitch across, then continue stuffing to within 1 inch (2.5cm) of open edge. Turn bottom edge of body ¼ inch (6mm) to inside and insert legs, with X marks matching at front and back. Machine-stitch across, securing the legs.

4 For the dress, measure and cut through folded pillowcase 15 inches (38cm) from the opening. Set aside for the skirt. Place sleeve and bodice front patterns on remaining pillowcase with long dash lines on fold. Cut 2 sleeves and 1 bodice front. Then cut 2 bodice backs.

With right sides facing, pin bodice backs to bodice front, matching shoulder edges. Stitch at shoulders only, with ¼ inch (6mm) seam allowance, up to black dot indicated on pattern. Turn neckline edge ¼ inch (6mm) to the wrong side, and stitch. Press the bodice, turning back edges ¼ inch (6mm) to wrong side.

Open each sleeve piece, hem bottom edges, and trim with ribbon. Sew gathering stitches along arched sleeve cap between **X** marks. Pin 1 sleeve to armhole of bodice, right sides facing, matching center of sleeve cap (highest point of arch) to shoulder seam and stitch together. Repeat on other side. Then fold sleeve from cap to hem, with right sides in, and align raw edges of sleeve and sides of bodice. Stitch bodice side and sleeve bottom in one continuous seam. Repeat.

To make the skirt, sew a gathering stitch along cut edge of pillowcase. Pin bodice backs so they overlap by ¼ inch (6mm) at center. With right sides facing, pin the skirt to the bodice and stitch together.

5 To finish, cut 5 inches (13cm) of ribbon and gather tightly into a rosette. Wrap remaining ribbon around the waist at seam; tack in front and tie in back. Tack rosette in place, using the green ribbon scrap for leaves. Sew on a snap to close the bodice backs at the top. For a necklace, thread beads onto a double strand of thread and knot ends.

# Days-of-the-Week Bedroom Set

**Sizes:** **Coverlet**, 56 x 78 inches (142 x 198cm), to fit a twin-size bed;
**Pillow Shams**, 33 x 18 inches (84 x 46cm);
**Throw Pillow**, 14 inches (36cm) square

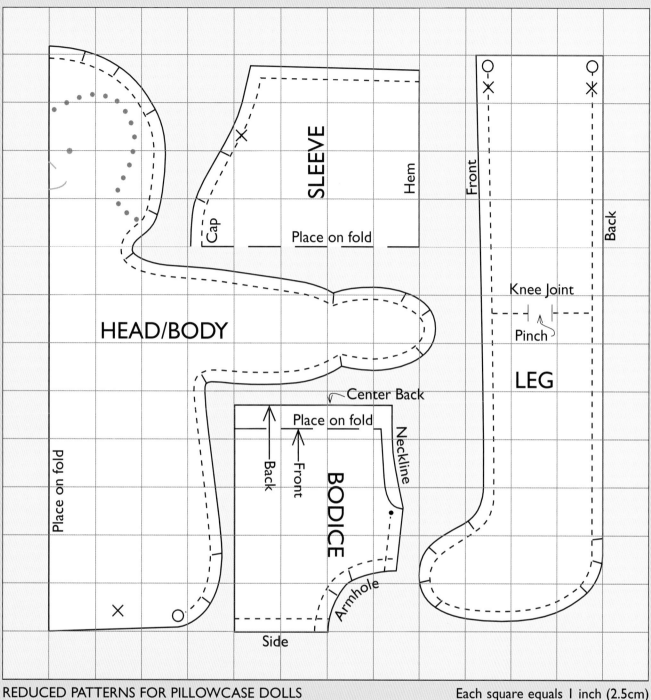

SLEEVE

Cap

Hem

Place on fold

HEAD/BODY

Place on fold

Center Back

Place on fold

Back

Front

BODICE

Neckline

Armhole

Side

Front

Back

Knee Joint

Pinch

LEG

REDUCED PATTERNS FOR PILLOWCASE DOLLS

Each square equals 1 inch (2.5cm)

## What You'll Need

**For Coverlet:**
- 12 days-of-the-week towels
- 8 new cotton dish towels, approximately 20 x 28 inches (51 x 71cm)
- Twin bed sheet, for backing
- Optional: coordinating embroidery floss

**For Each Pillow Sham:**
- 33 x 36 inch (84 x 92cm) day-of-the-week towel

**For Throw Pillow:**
- Day-of-the-week towel with striped border at ends, approximately 14 x 21 inches (36 x 54cm)

- 15-inch (38cm) square of matching fabric, for pillow back
- 14-inch (36cm) square pillow form

**For All:**
- Sewing thread to match fabrics

## What To Do

### COVERLET

Use ¼ inch (6mm) seam allowances throughout unless otherwise indicated. For background, remove hems from dish towels and press seams out flat. Pin 2 towels together, with right sides facing, matching short edges and any pattern in the fabric. Machine-sew together, and press seams open. Repeat to join 3 more pairs of towels to form a total of 4 long strips. Arrange strips alongside one another and stitch together, matching seams. Press seams open.

2 Pin background on sheet with right sides facing. (Trim sheet if needed.) Stitch around, leaving a 10-inch (26cm) opening. Clip across seam allowances at corners, and turn right side out. Turn open edges to inside and slipstitch closed. Press edges flat.

3 Cut days-of-the-week towels down, as necessary, for same-size squares or rectangles with embroidered design centered. (Some of the towels used had an embroidered edging on all sides that was lost when they were cut down. For consistency, we added matching embroidery to cut edges after hemming. Remaining towels were finished with an outline stitch.) Turn cut edges $^1$/$_2$ inch (13mm) to wrong side and embroider by hand or machine as desired.

4 Arrange days-of-the-week towels on background in four rows of three, with equal spaces between all rectangles and rows. Pin, then baste in place. Machine-stitch around each embroidered piece, $^1$/$_8$ inch (3mm) from edges. Remove basting threads.

### PILLOW SHAMS

1 Fold towel lengthwise in half with wrong side in. If working with smaller towels, use one for the front and another for the back.

2 Pin edges together and machine-stitch around, leaving one short side open.

### THROW PILLOW

1 Cut striped border, here about 3$^1$/$_2$ inches (9cm) deep, from top edge of towel. At bottom, embroidered end of towel, measure, mark, and cut a 14$^1$/$_2$-inch (37cm) square, with embroidery centered. Hem top edge. Pin striped border on top of square, with cut edge of border extending $^1$/$_2$ inch (13mm) beyond top of square, and side edges even. Pin and stitch along side edges to secure; this completes pillow top.

2 Place pillow top on matching fabric with right sides facing. Machine-stitch, $^1$/$_4$ inch (6mm) from edges on three sides. Cut across seam allowances at corners. Turn pillow cover to right side. Insert pillow form, then slipstitch open side closed.

## Morning, Noon & Evening Pillows

**Size:** As shown, 27 x 16$^1$/$_2$ inches (69 x 42cm)

### What You'll Need for Each

▶ Embroidered tea towel with border stripes
▶ 2 same-size kitchen towels, vintage or new, or fabric, for pillow top and back
▶ Sewing thread to match
▶ Polyester fiberfill, for stuffing

### What To Do

1 Frame the motif: If the tea towel has woven border stripes either lengthwise or at top and bottom, cut stripes and stitch around design area.

2 For pillow top, center the framed motif on a kitchen towel or rectangle of fabric. Pin, and topstitch $^1$/$_8$ inch (3mm) from edges all around.

3 Pin completed pillow top to same-size towel or fabric with right sides facing and edges even. Stitch all around, $^3$/$_8$ inch (1cm) from edges, leaving an opening for turning. Clip corners; turn to right side. Stuff plumply, and slipstitch open edges to close.

# Dresser Scarf Cat & Teddy Bear

**Sizes: Cat**, 8 inches (20.5cm) tall;
**Teddy Bear**, 11 inches (28cm) tall

## What You'll Need

▶ Embroidered dresser scarf—the one used here was
  14 x 40 inches (35.5 x 101.6cm)

▶ Sewing thread to match

▶ Polyester fiberfill, for stuffing

▶ ⁵/₈ yard (.6m) satin ribbon, ⁵/₈ inch-(15mm) wide

## What To Do

1 Enlarge patterns to full size and cut out. Arrange pattern pieces on ends of dresser scarf, using embroidery to best advantage. Piece fabric if necessary, so embroidery falls where you want it on the pattern; for example, fabric for the teddy bear's legs was seamed to the end of the dresser scarf, to allow embroidery to fall on the face. Pin patterns in place and cut out 1 cat body, cat tail, and teddy bear for fronts. Patterns include ¹/₄-inch (6mm) seam allowances. Use center of dresser scarf, or other fabric, to cut a same-size back for each front. Reverse cat patterns to cut backs.

2 Pin front and back pieces together in matching pairs, with right sides facing. Sew all around, leaving ¹/₄-inch (6mm) seam allowances and leaving areas unstitched between **O** marks as shown on patterns. Clip into seam allowances as indicated on patterns. Turn pieces to right side.

3 Stuff teddy bear and body and tail of cat with fiberfill. Turn in all open edges and slipstitch closed. For the cat, use a few stitches to tack straight end of tail to rump, at the seam. Match A and B points as shown on pattern. In the same way, secure top curve of tail to cat's back, matching C and D points. Tie a bow around each neck.

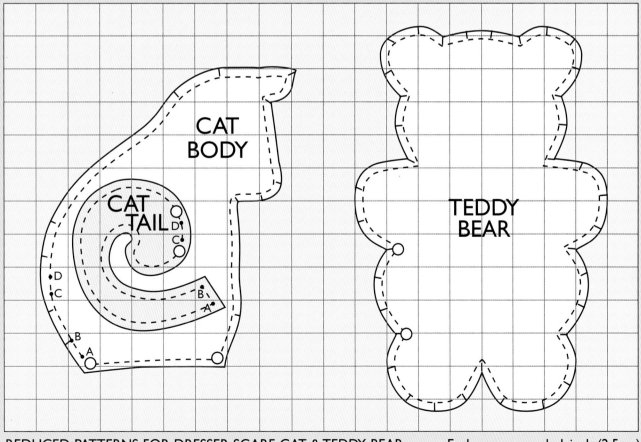

REDUCED PATTERNS FOR DRESSER SCARF CAT & TEDDY BEAR          Each square equals 1 inch (2.5cm)

# Christening Gown

**Size:** To fit infants up to 6 months

## What You'll Need

▶ Embroidered centerpiece cloth (ours has a drawnwork border), 23¹/₂ inches (60cm) square
▶ 7 embroidered coasters, 4³/₄ inches (12cm) square, not including fringe
▶ 1 yard (1m) white handkerchief-weight linen fabric, 54 inches (137cm) wide
▶ Sewing thread to match fabric
▶ 1 package white satin double-fold bias tape, ³/₄ inch (2cm) wide
▶ 4 small snaps

## What To Do

1 Begin with the linen fabric. For skirt, cut a 29-inch (74cm) length using the full width of the fabric. Then turn selvage edges 2 inches (5cm) to wrong side and press. Set aside. Enlarge patterns for bodice pieces. Cut 2 bodice backs. Fold remaining linen in half and place bodice-front pattern on fabric with long dash lines on fold. Cut out 1 bodice front.

2 For the skirt, bring pressed edges together, right sides facing, to create a center back seam. Stitch through all layers 1⁵/₈ inches (4cm) from pressed fold lines, stopping 5 inches (13cm) from one end for placket. Overlap the right edge of the placket with the left edge by 1 inch (2.5cm) and pin to secure. The placket will be the opening of the skirt where it joins the bodice opening. Now cut a 1¹/₄-inch (3cm) quarter circle or wedge at each side of the skirt top for armhole openings, which will extend below the bodice.

3 Unpin the placket. Sew gathering stitches along the top of the skirt, front and back, between bodice armholes. On each bodice back, hem center edge: Fold edges twice to wrong side along dotted lines and slipstitch. To attach bodice, pin bodice pieces to skirt, with right sides facing, and stitch together ³/₈ inch (1cm) from edges. Press seams toward skirt. Still with right sides facing, pin and then sew front and back bodice pieces together at shoulders. Press seams open and turn gown right side out.

4 For neckline, pin one long unfolded edge of bias tape to neckline, with right sides of tape and fabric facing, raw edges even, and ³/₈ inch (1cm) of bias tape extending at each end. Stitch along crease of

bias tape. Fold tape up and over to inside of gown, tucking tape ends in; slipstitch in place. Bind armholes in the same manner, starting and ending at bottom of armhole, with ends of tape neatly overlapping.

5 Launder and iron centerpiece cloth and coasters. Use embroidered centerpiece cloth as an apron front. Starting 2 inches (5cm) from center of one edge of cloth, pin pleats of equal size and spacing at both sides until this edge matches the width of the front where bodice and skirt join. Press pleats flat. Stitch across cloth to secure pleats, first along top edge and again 2 inches (5cm) below. To attach apron to gown, pin pleated edge at bodice/skirt seam, folding the top corners into the armholes. Machine or hand-stitch in place.

6 To hand-sew coasters to gown, use small slipstitches at edges to secure in place. How you position coasters exactly will depend on how many you have to work with. In this case, coasters are used for each sleeve, on the bodice, and apron center and edge. First, center a coaster diagonally on bodice front and stitch in place. Then, to form a sleeve, fold 1 coaster diagonally in half. Crease and unfold. Pin, with underside of crease lining up along a shoulder seam and with 1 inch (2.5cm) of coaster corner tucked inside neckline. Coaster/sleeve will drape beyond armhole as shown in photo. Repeat to make second sleeve. Now position 1 coaster in center of apron, on the diagonal, and stitch, being careful to sew to apron layer only. Stitch top points of remaining 3 coasters to apron edge.

7 Test-fit christening gown on infant. Determine overlap of back opening for best fit. Mark positions for snaps to close bodice and skirt placket and sew on. Hem skirt.

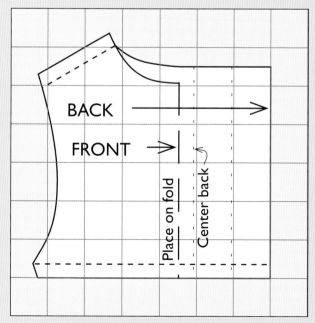

## REDUCED PATTERN FOR GOWN BODICE
Each square equals 1 inch (2.5cm)

# Guest-Towel Pillows

**Size:** Approximately 19 x 12 inches (48 x 30cm)

## What You'll Need for Each

▶ Embroidered guest towel, approximately 17 inches (43cm) wide

▶ 1³/₈ yards (1.3m) grosgrain Swiss dot ribbon,
  ⁵/₈ inch (15mm) wide, for bows at sides

▶ ³/₈ yard (.35m) cotton or cotton blend fabric,
  44–45 inches (115cm) wide, for pillow cover

▶ Sewing thread to match fabrics

▶ Polyester fiberfill, for stuffing

## What To Do

1 Make the pillow sleeve: Fold guest towel to display the embroidered design to best advantage. In some instances, the ends will overlap on the front. On one pillow, the towel is arranged to show two scalloped borders. Pin top and bottom edges of guest towel together as planned. Use slipstitches to hand-sew an overlapped edge; hand- or machine-sew a seam with a small running stitch; use overcast stitches to butt edges together.

2 For side bows, cut 2 or 4 pairs of ribbon strands in 12-inch (31cm) lengths. Fold one end of each strand under and tack to sides of the guest towel, one in front and one in back.

3 For the pillow insert, first lay the sleeve out flat. Add 3 inches (7.5cm) to measurement of long edges, and 1 inch (2.5cm) to measurement of short edges; cut 2 rectangles from fabric to these dimensions. Pin fabric rectangles together, with right sides facing. Machine-stitch around, ¹/₂ inch (13mm) from edges, leaving a 4-inch (10cm) opening in center of one long edge. Clip into seam allowances at corners. Turn pillow insert to right side and stuff; slipstitch opening closed. Slide sleeve over pillow insert and tie ribbon into bows.

# Window Panel

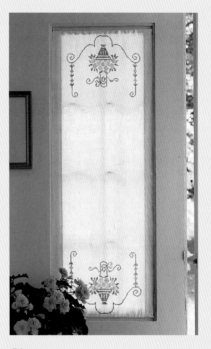

**Size:** To fit

## What You'll Need

▶ Embroidered dresser scarf at
  least as long as area to be
  covered—the one used here was
  26 x 70 inches (66 x 178cm)

▶ Sewing thread to match

▶ Optional: Wide ribbon

▶ Sash or tension rods, 1 pair per panel

## What To Do

1 Install sash or tension rods at top and bottom of window if necessary. Measure distance between them.

2 If dresser scarf is same distance, sew ribbon casings to wrong side at short ends. If dresser scarf is 2 inches (5cm) longer, fold each end 1 inch (2.5cm) to wrong side for casings and stitch. If dresser scarf is more than 2 inches (5cm) longer, make a casing at one end, for panel bottom, and fold the remainder of the scarf over the top rod toward the front; stitch across for top casing.

## Guest-Book Cover

**Size:** 6 x 9 inches (15 x 23cm), or to fit

### What You'll Need

▶ Embroidered guest towel with a decorative edging—ours measured 17 x 19¹/₂ inches (43 x 50cm)

▶ Small book—this one is a small loose-leaf binder, 5¹/₂ x 8 inches (14 x 20.5cm)

▶ Small piece of fusible batting

▶ 1 yard (1m) of twisted cord, for trim

▶ Sewing thread to match guest towel and twisted cord

### What To Do

1 Cut towel crosswise in half, and lay halves side by side, with embroidered area on the right and finished edges along bottom. Pin halves together, with right sides facing and seam along adjacent sides, to make a horizontal rectangle. Unfold, and press seam open.

2 To pad front cover, arrange towel, right side up, around book, with decorative edging extending ¹/₂ inch (13mm) at the bottom and embroidery centered. Outline area for front cover with pins. Measure and cut fusible batting to fit within pins. Fuse batting to wrong side of towel, removing pins as you iron.

3 To fit cover, position towel around book again as in Step 2. Trim top edge of towel to extend ¹/₂ inch (13mm) above top of book. Turn this ¹/₂ inch (13mm) under, toward book; press; and hem. Then, as shown in diagram, fold remaining fabric at front and back covers to the inside for pockets. (Trim to fit if necessary, and turn cut edges under and hem.) If it's not necessary to cut fabric, selvage edges of towel do not need to be hemmed.

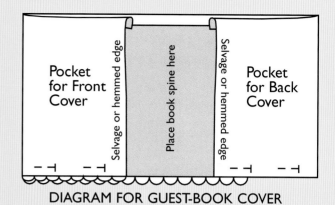

Pocket for Front Cover

Selvage or hemmed edge

Place book spine here

Selvage or hemmed edge

Pocket for Back Cover

**DIAGRAM FOR GUEST-BOOK COVER**

4 To complete assembly, pin book cover snugly along bottom edge. Make sure that book can be opened and closed and make adjustments as necessary. Remove cover from book and slipstitch along line of pins. Starting at bottom front edge, slipstitch twisted cord up the side, across top, and down the other side edge. Use thread to match cord.

## Chair-Back Cover & Place Mats

**Sizes: Chair-Back Cover,** to fit most straight-back wood chairs; **Place Mats,** approximately 17¹/₂ x 27 inches (44 x 69cm)

### What You'll Need

▶ Kitchen towels with an embroidered motif and/or lettering; as shown, approximately 17¹/₂ x 27 inches (44 x 69cm)

▶ ¹/₂ yard (.5m) cotton or cotton blend fabric, 44–45 inches wide (114cm), for lining

▶ Sewing thread

▶ Fusible batting

**For Chair-Back Cover:**

▶ 1 package double-fold bias tape, ¹/₂ inch (13mm) wide, for ties

## What To Do

1 For chair-back cover, drape towel over top of chair, with embroidery at back. If towel is wider than chair back, turn ends to wrong side, pin, and press. Cut batting same size and fuse to wrong side.

2 For place mats, arrange towel on table with embroidered area hanging off the edge. Anchor towel with a plate and determine how much of towel will serve as a place mat, and how much will be overhang. Pin along towel at table's edge. Cut batting to match area marked by pins and fuse in place to wrong side of towel.

3 To line chair-back and/or place mats, cut out lining fabric ¹/₂ inch (13mm) larger all around than batting and press these seam allowances to wrong side. Place lining over batting, with wrong sides facing, and pin generously. Topstitch all around by machine, ¹/₈ inch (3mm) from edges.

4 To make chair-back ties, cut bias tape into four 13¹/₂-inch (34cm) lengths. Turn in one end of each length ¹/₄ inch (6mm), and slipstitch or topstitch along all edges. Pin raw ends of ties to wrong side of towel, so ties extend out in pairs: 2 inches (5cm) from top of chair and again 12 inches (31cm) below, or where appropriate to secure slipcover on your chair. Baste in place.

## Tea Cozy

**Size:** 14¹/₂ x 9¹/₂ inches (37 x 24cm) high

## What You'll Need

▶ Tea towel at least 15 inches (38cm) wide
▶ ³/₈ yard (.35m) coordinating fabric, for lining
▶ Sewing thread to match

▶ Fusible batting
▶ 1 yard (1m) of twisted cord, for trim
▶ Large sheet of tracing paper or tissue paper and 14–inch (36cm) dinner plate or compass for pattern

## What To Do

1 Referring to the diagram, draw a pattern on paper. Use a plate or compass to produce a neat curve, a ruler to mark straight lines. Pattern includes ¹/₄-inch (6mm) seam allowances; use these throughout.

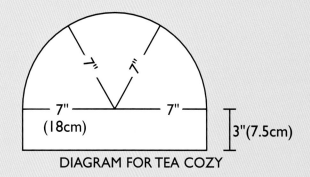

7"
7"
7" (18cm) — 7"
3"(7.5cm)

**DIAGRAM FOR TEA COZY**

2 Lay pattern over embroidered design and border of towel, and arrange to best advantage. Pin pattern in place and cut out for tea cozy front. Cut a same-size piece from the opposite end of the towel, for cozy back, plus 2 same-size pieces each from lining fabric and batting. For the top loop of cozy, cut a 2¹/₂ x 3-inch (7 x 8cm) rectangle from remaining towel fabric; ours is cut from a remaining border.

3 Fold loop piece lengthwise in half, right side in. Stitch along long edges, forming a tube. Turn tube right side out and press flat with seam centered. Pin loop, folded crosswise and seam inside, to center top of tea cozy front, with raw edges even. Pin front and back pieces together, with right sides facing. Machine-stitch around outside edge. Clip into seam allowance along curves and turn tea cozy to right side.

4 Trim seam allowances from batting pieces, then center one on wrong side of each lining piece and fuse in place. Pin lining pieces together, with right sides facing, and stitch around curved edge. Pin tea cozy and lining together with right sides facing, raw edges even, and seams matching. Stitch around, leaving a 6-inch (15cm) opening along center back. Turn tea cozy to right side, and slip lining inside. Turn open edges in and slipstitch closed.

5 Slipstitch twisted cord along side and top seam, to the front of the loop; turn unfinished end of cord under and wrap with thread to secure.

# Eyeglass Case

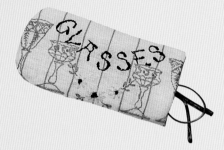

**Size:** $3^3/_4$ x 7 inches (9.5 x 18cm)

## What You'll Need

▶ Kitchen towel (we used one with "glasses" embroidered on it)

▶ 8 x 9-inch (21 x 23cm) rectangle of cotton fabric, for lining

▶ 8 x 9-inch (21 x 23cm) rectangle of fusible batting

▶ Sewing thread to match towel

▶ Tracing paper, pencil, ruler

## What To Do

1 Make a pattern: On the edges of a sheet of tracing paper, mark a $4^1/_2$ x $7^3/_4$-inch (11.5 x 20cm) rectangle—which includes $^3/_8$-inch (1cm) seam allowances. Or, trace around an existing case and add $^3/_8$-inch (1cm) seam allowances. Cut out. Use a pencil to gracefully round the corners at one end; cut out.

2 Place pattern on towel, centering embroidery. Pin in place and cut out. Remove pattern, and use it to cut another piece from towel for back of case plus 2 pieces for lining and 2 pieces from batting. Trim $^3/_8$ inch (1cm) from batting pieces.

3 Place front and back pieces together, right sides facing and edges even, and stitch around $^3/_8$ inch (1cm) from edges, leaving the short straight edge open. Fuse a batting piece to the center of each lining piece, on the wrong side. Place lining pieces together, right sides facing, and stitch same as for front and back. Clip into seam allowances along curves on both case exterior and lining pieces. Turn the case exterior but not the lining to right side. Insert the lining, matching seams. Turn open edges to their wrong side: exterior fabric $^1/_4$ inch (6mm) and lining $^3/_8$ inch (1cm). Pin these folded edges together, and slipstitch along the foldline of the lining to secure it in place.

# "Baby" Curtain

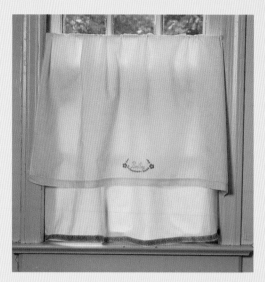

**Size:** To fit most standard casement windows

## What You'll Need

▶ Crib sheet with an embroidered border—
the one used here was 35 x 47 inches (89 x 119cm)

▶ 1 inch (2.5cm)-wide ribbon, for trim

▶ Sewing thread to match

▶ $^3/_4$-inch (2cm) round hook-and-loop fasteners, such as Velcro® coins

## What To Do

1 Fold crib sheet crosswise, off-center, and hold up to the window with the bottom edge just meeting the window sill. Curtain will feature this two-tiered effect. Determine proper height for a rod. Install a sash rod for an outside mount, or adjust a tension rod to fit the space for an inset mount.

2 Measure width of crib sheet. Cut ribbon 1 inch (2.5cm) longer than this measurement and turn ends $^1/_2$ inch (13mm) to wrong side. Pin ribbon to wrong side of crib sheet, flush with the bottom edge; stitch in place.

3 To hold curtain in place, attach corresponding hook-and-loop fasteners a short distance below rod.

# "Sugar" & "Sweets to the Sweet" Bibs

**Sizes:** **"Sugar" bib**, 11 inches (28cm) wide by 12¹/₂ inches (32cm) long, to fit babies and toddlers up to 3 years of age; **"Sweets" bib**, 7¹/₄ inches (18.5cm) wide by 8¹/₄ inches (21cm) long, not including fringe, to fit infants up to 6 months of age

## What You'll Need

**For "Sugar" Bib:**

▶ Embroidered doily—this one was intended to go under a sugar bowl

▶ Coordinating cotton fabric, 13¹/₂ x 23 inches (35 x 59cm)

▶ Large sheet of tracing paper or tissue paper

**For "Sweets" Bib:**

▶ Cloth napkin with embroidery at one corner and fringed or otherwise finished edges, at least 16 inches (41cm) square, not including fringe

**For Either Bib:**

▶ 1 package of double-fold bias tape

▶ Sewing thread

## What To Do

1 Enlarge the half pattern. Place "Sugar" bib pattern on folded paper, with long dash lines along fold. Cut out. Open pattern.

2 For "Sugar" bib, fold fabric crosswise in half to form an 11¹/₂ x 13¹/₂-inch (30 x 35cm) rectangle, then crosswise in half again. Pin actual-size half pattern on fabric with long dash lines along double fold. Cut out fabric pieces for bib front and back. For bib front, center embroidered doily on right side of one bib piece. Slipstitch edges in place, using thread to match doily edges. Pin bib pieces together, with wrong sides facing, and stitch around, close to all raw edges.

3 For "Sweets" bib, fold napkin diagonally in half, with embroidery face up in a corner opposite the fold. Pin layers of folded fabric

together. Position pattern on napkin, with embroidered corner center front, and pin in place. Cut out along all but fringed edges. Remove pattern, then stitch 2 napkin layers together all around, close to edges.

4 Bind raw edges all around "Sugar" bib and along shoulders of "Sweets" bib as follows, saving neckline for last: Cut bias tape to length of edge(s) to be bound, adding ¹/₄ inch (6mm) for tucking under visible ends. Open double-fold bias tape and pin, with right sides facing, to raw edges of bib front. Machine-stitch along crease of tape ¹/₄ inch (6mm) from edges. Fold tape over edge, tucking ends in, and pin to back of bib. Slipstitch opposite long edges of tape in place. To bind necklines, cut a piece of bias tape 1 yard (1m) long. Turn in ¹/₄ inch (6mm) at each end and slipstitch to secure. Center unfolded tape on bib neckline and pin in place. Stitch along neckline in same manner as before, but continue slipstitches out to each end, for ties.

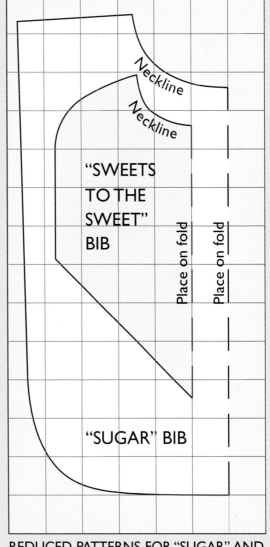

**REDUCED PATTERNS FOR "SUGAR" AND "SWEETS TO THE SWEET" BIBS**
Each square equals 1 inch (2.5cm)

# Chapter Two

# *Chenille*

Stores from New York to Los Angeles are quickly selling out of toys and pillows made from old chenille. And these items sell for as much as $150. However, smart shoppers who buy slightly damaged bedspreads can easily stitch up their own clever gifts and accessories.

Two red-and-white chenille bedspreads combine to make up this pillow set. One floral pattern is used on the settee seat cushion and two reversible pillows. A smaller rosebud or "hobnail" pattern is made into a heart and a bolster.

*L*ike souvenir birchbark canoes, printed burlap sachets stuffed with pine needles, and marshmallows toasted on an open fire, chenille bedspreads—often associated with summer vacations and lakeside cottages—awaken happy childhood memories.

Although considered garish—and even tacky—until recently, these campy bedcovers are now coveted, collectible, and chic. Less-than-perfect chenille bedspreads are affordable and available at flea markets and thrift shops. Buyers are rewarded with generous-size, all-cotton, machine-washable fabric.

## A LITTLE HISTORY

Tufted bedspreads date back to colonial times when the wick for candles was used to mend cloth. Pioneer women discovered that darning could become decorative by clipping, tying, and fluffing the ends to make a "tuft." A group of tufts could create a design.

Thanks to the research and records of the Whitfield-Murray Historical Society in Dalton,

**Children will love to cuddle up with these adorable chenille and gingham toys. The elephant can double as a pillow at nap time.**

Georgia, we are able to trace the evolution of traditional white-on-white New England candle-wicking to the explosively colored commercial bedspreads we now know as chenille.

It all started with a young woman named Catherine Evans. Catherine went to visit her cousin in nearby McCuthey, Georgia, and admired a family heirloom, a tufted bedspread. She promised herself that she'd make one like it some day. And, in 1895, at the age of fifteen she did just that. Catherine sharpened the blunt end of her mother's bodkin needle to make a tool and then she drew a pattern on unbleached muslin and started sewing looped stitches. She clipped each stitch with scissors to create an individual tuft. Over fifty years later, in an interview for *Conasauga* magazine, Catherine confided, "It took so long to make that spread that it was terribly soiled by the time it was finished. I was disappointed to have to ruin it by laundering it, but when I hung it in the sun, the tufts became snowy fluffs and the spread was beautiful. " Soon, she made another as a wedding gift for her brother and then another—and another—as her work became admired and known. Her floral patterns were inspired by curtains, carpets, and china. Geometric designs were derived from quilts. Catherine charged $2.50 for the first spread that she sold: Stitched on seamed flour sacks, the materials had cost $1.25.

For ten years, these tufted spreads were pretty much a one-woman business although Catherine hired friends and relatives to help meet the demand. Little did she know that this homespun craft would change the future of her hometown of Dalton, Georgia, and become a piece of Americana not to mention the start of a billion-dollar tufted-textile industry.

By the 1920s, other women (and their husbands) got into the act of making and distributing these spreads. There was more than enough work for everyone. Department stores, including John Wanamaker's in New York, placed large orders. Business continued to thrive even during the Depression and Dalton became known as the "Bedspread Capital of the World."

One full-size bedspread is all that was needed for a
baby quilt, pillow, lamp shade, and toys. The center
medallion was used for this fluffy quilt.

Plush and densely tufted designs are shown to the best advantage on this sunny chenille travel set. In addition to a tote and duffel bag, you could also add a garment bag.

By the 1930s, machines that could stitch long continuous strips of tufting were developed and the word chenille came into use. (*Chenille* is the French word for "caterpillar" and you can certainly see the resemblance to these fuzzy creatures in the rows of tufted stitches.) The work moved into factories and spreads were mass-produced.

Highway 41, a 150-mile stretch along Georgia's southern border, from Tennessee to Florida, became known as "Bedspread Row" or "Peacock Alley"—after a popular pattern. Tourists flocked there for the dazzling spreads displayed at roadside stands or drying on clotheslines. These spreads from the 1930s, 1940s, and 1950s are the ones we recognize and find at flea markets today.

### SHOPPING FOR CHENILLE

Twin and full-size bedspreads are good buys as they provide the most yardage. In the 1950s, floor-length spreads that measured 108 inches (276.5cm) were introduced. Look for densely tufted areas and medallion centers for larger projects. Individual motifs and interesting border areas make up into a variety of pillow shapes. Overall

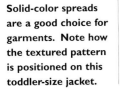

**Solid-color spreads are a good choice for garments. Note how the textured pattern is positioned on this toddler-size jacket.**

patterns, including florals, are the most plentiful and the most versatile.

When shopping for spreads, the type of damage you're most likely to find is small holes, tears, and wear around the edges. Open the spread completely, inspect both sides for imperfections, and hold it up to the light to see what holes exist and where they are. If a chenille bedspread has a wonderful heart-patterned border that will make several stunning bolster pillows, it doesn't matter if the center is badly ripped. If there are appealing designs in just the corners and even if only two are in good shape—but the price is right—there can still be enough fabric for a vest or a tote bag. None of the bedspreads purchased for this chapter cost more than $35.

Serious collectors seek out bedspreads featuring Roy Rogers and Trigger, Dale Evans, or Hopalong Cassidy. These can sell for as much as $650, if they are in excellent condition. (Don't confuse them with generic cowboy spreads, which are considerably less valuable.) Chances are you won't come across these at flea markets but rather at vintage textiles dealers.

Originally made from leftover bits of colored yarns, probably the most famous (and prized) designs are the ones featuring peacocks. They come in a number of combinations but usually with one or two peacocks down the center of the spread and perhaps a pair across the top. In good condition, a spectacular peacock spread can cost $300. I bought a wonderfully flashy one in magenta and purples for only $25. It was a bargain because it was frayed around the edges. Instead of cutting it up, however, it's on my bed—tatters and all. When you are about to buy a peacock-pattern spread, think about how you intend to use it. Pillows are not a good idea as you don't want to behead the birds by cutting into them. Curtains can be a good idea since you will be able to take advantage of the two tall peacocks (one on each curtain) and use the section at the top for a matching valance. Peacocks also fit down the back of a bathrobe.

White and pastel crib-size spreads may feature playful lambs, puppies, kittens, clowns, hearts, baby blocks, or other toys. Harder to find

It only takes a corner of a bedspread to cover this lamp shade. Ball fringe comes from the spread as well.

and, therefore, more expensive, these smaller spreads offer fewer opportunities for crafters. Expect to pay as much as $50, or even more for ones in reasonable condition. However, they can be charming as a wall hanging in a child's room, a bunting, or a carriage cover.

Chenille curtains were also manufactured but you'll find that these pieces usually aren't large enough for many projects.

### TIPS TO REMEMBER

When working with any vintage textiles, it's important to launder them first. Chenille spreads were made to be machine-washed. You'll find that not only will the colors brighten up (you'll want to do this before purchasing any matching trims) but the tufting will fluff up considerably, as Catherine Evans discovered with her first bedspread.

Often chenille spreads come with an edging which could be fringe, ball fringe, or even a fabric ruffle. Carefully remove these trims and reapply them to your finished projects or save for later use. It's also possible to purchase edgings that have been cut from other spreads at flea markets: I bought a bag of more than 20 yards of assorted lengths of this ball fringe for $5.00. While we're on the subject of edges, you'll find rounded corners, scalloped edges, or plain ones. Think about your intended project. Plain edges are easier to hem. Rounded corners might present a challenge if you have to cut through one side. What will happen if you have to cut into a scalloped edge?

Tips to remember when sewing chenille projects: Draw your pattern on the wrong (nontufted side) of the fabric and pay attention to the direction of the tufted rows if you wish to match them up. Iron the back side and on a padded surface. If tufts get caught up in stitched seams, use a tapestry needle or simply a pin to pull them out.

Whatever you decide to make from chenille, the results are almost guaranteed to elicit comforting feelings of nostalgia.

Even a small section of an overall design, an individual motif, or an attractive border can be enough to inspire a one-of-a-kind throw pillow.

For a truly retro look, try chenille in the shower (over a liner, of course). There was enough fabric in this 1950s spread to make a matching valance.

# Settee Cushion

**Size:** To fit

## What You'll Need

▶ Chenille bedspread
▶ Sewing thread to match
▶ Existing cushion or 3–4 bags of polyester fiberfill
▶ Zipper to fit one short side of cushion
▶ Pencil; large sheet of brown paper; yardstick
▶ Sewing machine with zipper foot attachment

## What To Do

To make a pattern, spread a large sheet of paper over bottom of seat and trace around seat, or trace existing cushion: Keep pencil perpendicular to seat. Remove paper and use yardstick to even edges; cut out. Pin pattern for cushion top to bedspread, arranging chenille motifs to best advantage. Adding ½ inch (13mm) all around for seam allowances, cut out cushion top. Cut out an identical piece for bottom of cushion.

For boxing strips, measure front, back, and side edges of cushion top. From remaining chenille fabric, cut strips 4½ inches (11cm) wide or 1 inch (2.5cm) wider than depth of existing cushion, and 1 inch (2.5cm) longer than front, back, and 1 side. For zipper end, cut 2 boxing strips equal to the length of the opposite side. For front

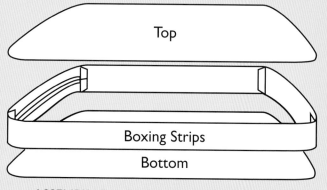

ASSEMBLY DIAGRAM FOR SETTEE CUSHION

boxing strip, try to match pattern to top. Follow manufacturer's instructions on the zipper package to insert a zipper between these duplicate strips, then trim the joined strip so it matches the other strips in width, with the zipper centered lengthwise.

2 For all stitching, pin pieces together with right sides facing and edges even. Stitch, leaving ½-inch (13mm) seam allowances. First, stitch short edges of all the boxing strips together to make a ring. Press seams toward back of cushion. Pin cushion top to 1 long edge of boxing strip ring, matching corresponding edges and placing seams at corners; stitch. Pin and stitch cushion bottom to opposite long edge of ring in same manner. Clip into seam allowances at corners and along curves, as necessary. Turn cushion cover to right side. Insert cushion or stuff plumply with fiberfill.

# Heart Pillow

**Size:** 16 inches (41cm) high and wide

## What You'll Need

▶ Fabric from a chenille bedspread: two 17-inch (43cm) squares
▶ Sewing thread to match fabric
▶ Polyester fiberfill
▶ Pencil; large sheet of paper; compass

## What To Do

For pattern, follow diagram to draw a half heart on paper folded in half. Use a compass to draw the half circle with a 4-inch (10cm) radius at top. Unfold paper; if desired, adjust heart shape. Pin pattern to chenille fabric, centering any motif in fabric if possible. Adding ¼ inch (6mm) for seam allowances all around, cut out heart shape for pillow top. Repeat for pillow back.

2 Pin pillow top on back with right sides facing and edges even. Machine-stitch all around, ¼ inch (6mm) from edges, leaving a 4-inch (10cm) opening along a straight edge. Cut across seam

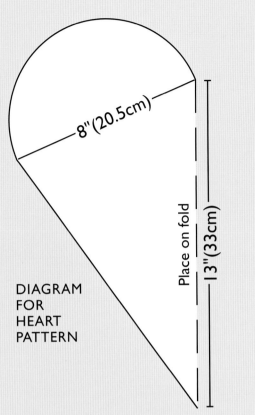

8" (20.5cm)

Place on fold

13"(33cm)

DIAGRAM
FOR
HEART
PATTERN

## What To Do

1 For patterns, mark on tracing paper and cut out an 18 x 25-inch (46 x 63.5cm) rectangle and, using a compass, a circle with a $4^{7}/_{8}$-inch (12.5cm) radius. Patterns include $^{1}/_{2}$-inch (13mm) seam allowances. Pin patterns on chenille fabric with design areas centered. Cut out 1 rectangle and 2 circles.

2 To assemble, pin pieces together with right sides facing and raw edges even. Stitch $^{1}/_{2}$ inch (13mm) from edges. Begin by bringing short edges of rectangle together and stitching, leaving a 5-inch (12.5cm) opening for turning at the center. Pin a circle at either end; stitch. Clip into seam allowances along curves and turn to right side. Stuff plumply, turn open edges to inside, and slipstitch to close.

3 Hand-stitch ball fringe at either end of bolster with pompons facing out, ends neatly overlapped, and seams at bolster ends concealed.

## Knife-Edge Pillows

allowances at bottom corner; clip into seam allowances at top angle and along curves. Turn pillow cover to right side. Stuff with fiberfill. Turn open edges to inside and slipstitch closed.

## Bolster Pillow

**Size:** Approximately 17 inches (43cm) long and 8 inches (20cm) in diameter

## What You'll Need

▶ 1 square yard (1m) fabric from a chenille bedspread
▶ Sewing thread to match fabric
▶ Polyester fiberfill
▶ $1^{1}/_{2}$ yards (1.4m) old or new ball fringe
▶ Pencil; tracing paper; compass

**Sizes: Red-and-White Pillows, on loveseat,**
14 inches (35.5cm) square;
**Blue-and-White Pillow,** 16 inches (41cm) square;
**Rectangular Pillow, with green ball fringe,**
12 x 13 inches (30.5 x 33cm)

## What You'll Need

- Fabric sections from chenille bedspreads
- Sewing thread to match fabric
- Polyester fiberfill or appropriately sized pillow form
- For rectangular pillow: 1 1/2 yards (1.4m) old or new cotton ball fringe
- Pencil; large sheet of tracing paper; clear quilter's ruler or T-square

## What To Do

1 Refer to the pillow-making section of the General Directions, Chapter Eight. Make a closed pillow, or one with an overlapped back. If you wish to add a trim, read Step 2 before assembling the pillow.

2 To trim with ball fringe, pin ball fringe around right side of pillow top, with straight edge of ball fringe even with raw edge of pillow top. Use a zipper foot attachment to machine-baste in place, close to inside edges of ball-fringe tape. When assembling pillow, machine-stitch just inside of previous basting.

## Baby Quilt Set

**Sizes: Quilt,** 46 x 57 inches (117 x 145cm); **Pillow,** 16 inches (41cm) high and wide

## What You'll Need

- Full-size chenille bedspread
- Flat, twin-size cotton sheet or 1 1/2 yards (1.4m) fabric 54 inches (137cm) wide, for backing
- Sewing thread to match bedspread and backing fabric
- Poly-fil® Hi-Loft® Batting, 72 x 90 inches (183 x 229cm)

**For Pillow:**
- Polyester fiberfill, for stuffing
- Optional: 1 1/2 yards (1.4m) cotton piping cord 1/2 inch (13mm) in

diameter, and 1/2 yard (.5m) gingham cotton fabric, for piping; washable fabric glue, for appliqué.

## What To Do

### QUILT

1 For quilt top, cut a 47 x 58 inch (120 x 148cm) rectangle from chenille bedspread, centering medallion of fabric. Cut fabric for backing and batting to same size.

2 To assemble quilt, spread backing wrong side up on a flat surface, with batting on top. Pin and baste together. Turn backing right side up and place quilt top, wrong side up, on top. Stitch around 1/2 inch (13mm) from raw edges, leaving about 12 inches (30.5cm) open for turning. Trim seams to 1/4 inch (6mm) and clip across seam allowances at corners. Turn quilt to right side, and slipstitch opening closed.

3 To quilt, work from the center and baste outward in all directions. Starting at center and working outward, machine-quilt along design lines in chenille fabric, or as desired.

### HEART PILLOW

1 Make heart pillow following directions on page 40. Use a section of the bedspread with an interesting motif or cut out a design and appliqué it in place. Cut the motif 1/8 inch (3mm) beyond tufting threads. Stitch or use fabric glue to apply motif to center of pillow top; let glue dry before assembling pillow.

2 Turn to the section on making trims in the General Directions, Chapter Eight. Make and add piping, covering cotton piping cord with gingham fabric.

## Bunny & Elephant

**Sizes: Bunny,** 14 inches (35.5cm) tall, not including floppy 7-inch (18cm)-long ears; **Elephant,** 9 inches (23cm) tall and 13 inches (33cm) long

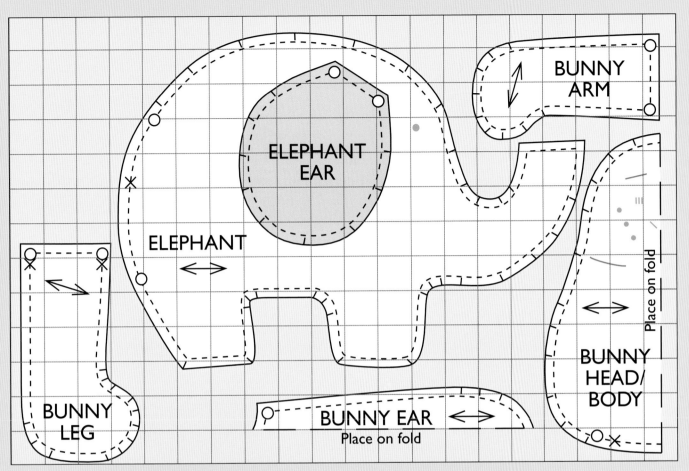

**REDUCED PATTERNS FOR BUNNY AND ELEPHANT**

Each square equals 1 inch (2.5cm)

## What You'll Need

▶ Section from a chenille bedspread totaling approximately 18 inches (46cm) square

▶ Sewing thread to match

▶ Small amount of cotton gingham fabric

▶ Polyester fiberfill, for stuffing

▶ Six-strand embroidery floss, for facial features

▶ Scrap of ribbon or fabric, for bunny's bow

▶ 5 inches (12.5cm) satin ribbon $^3/_8$-inch (10mm) wide, for elephant's tail

▶ Sewing and embroidery needles

## What To Do

**1** Enlarge patterns to full size and cut out. Complete half patterns for the bunny head/body and ear as follows: Fold tracing paper in half, lay the long dash lines of the pattern on the fold, trace the pattern, cut it out, and unfold the complete pattern. When placing patterns on chenille fabric, keep arrows parallel to any design-line stripes in fabric. Patterns include $^1/_4$-inch (6mm) seam allowances.

**2** For the bunny, cut out the following from chenille fabric, reversing the pattern to create mirror images for second and fourth arm and leg pieces: 2 head/body pieces; 4 each, ears, arms, legs. From gingham fabric, cut out a $3^1/_2$ x $34^1/_2$-inch (9 x 88cm) rectangle for ruffled collar.

For the elephant, cut 2 body pieces, reversing pattern for second piece, and 2 ears from chenille. Also cut 2 ears from gingham fabric.

**3** Refer to the short blue lines in the pattern markings to embroider the bunny's face. Using 4 strands of embroidery floss in an embroidery needle, make 3 straight stitches all alongside each other for eyes and 2 straight stitches for nose. For whiskers, insert needle into face at one side of nose, as indicated by 3 blue dots, and emerge on the other side of the nose; leave ends $2^1/_2$ inches (6.5cm) long on each side. On elephant, embroider a French knot on each side of the head for eyes.

**4** To assemble, pin pieces together in matching pairs with right sides facing, matching edges to be joined. Sew $^1/_4$ inch (6mm) from edges, leaving open between **O** marks as indicated on patterns. Clip into the seam allowances along curves and at angles, as indicated on patterns. Turn pieces right side out through openings. Use eraser end of a pencil to push ears, trunk, arms, and legs through, and to push stuffing into hard-to-reach areas. Stuff all but ears with fiberfill. Unless otherwise indicated, turn open edges $1/4$ inch (6mm) to inside and slipstitch closed.

**5** For the bunny, assemble body, 2 arms, 2 legs, and 2 ears. Stuff body, arms, and legs to within 1 inch of openings. Turn ends of ears and arms to inside and slipstitch to secure. Pin ears to back of head as indicated by red lines. Pin tops of arms as indicated by red lines on sides of body front. Slipstitch these pieces securely in place. Insert tops of legs into bottom of body, with leg seams at center and **X** points matching. Machine-stitch across body to close and secure legs.

For ruffled collar, make a narrow hem all around the gingham fabric strip. Gather one long edge and tie thread ends around neck. Tie a knot in the center of a 1 x 4-inch (2.5 x 10cm) scrap of fabric or ribbon; tack to center top of collar.

**6** For the elephant, assemble body pieces. Fold ribbon scrap crosswise in half and insert ends at **X** mark, for tail, before slipstitching body closed. Stitch a gingham ear to each chenille ear. Turn open edges to inside and press lightly. Position on either side of body as indicated on pattern; slipstitch straight edges in place.

## Tote Bag

**Size:** 21 x 17 x 3$1/2$ inches (53 x 43 x 9cm)

## What You'll Need

▶ Chenille bedspread—we made both the tote and duffel bags from a full-size bedspread

▶ 2 yards (2m) lining fabric

▶ Sewing thread to match fabrics

▶ 2 yards (2m) fusible batting

▶ 1$1/2$ yards (1.4m) heavyweight interfacing or buckram

## What To Do

**1** Begin by cutting rectangles from chenille bedspread, centering or positioning motifs in fabric to best advantage: two 22 x 19 inches (56 x 48.5cm) for front and back, two 5 x 19 inches (13 x 48cm) for sides, one 22 x 5 inches (56 x 12.5cm) for bottom, and two 3 x 15 inches (7.5 x 38cm) for handles. Measurements include $1/2$-inch (13mm) seam allowances. Cut interfacing and lining to same size for all but bottom piece. Cut fusible batting for front, back, and straps $1/2$ inch (13mm) smaller all around than corresponding chenille pieces.

**2** Centering, fuse batting to wrong side of corresponding chenille pieces. Baste interfacing to wrong side of front and back lining pieces.

**3** To assemble, pin chenille front, bottom, and back pieces together with right sides facing and edges even. Seam along long edges, with $1/2$-inch (13mm) seam allowances. With right sides facing, pin joined front/bottom/back around side pieces, matching edges and placing seams at corners. Stitch all around; clip into seam allowance at corners. Turn top edges $1/2$ inch (13mm) to wrong side and press.

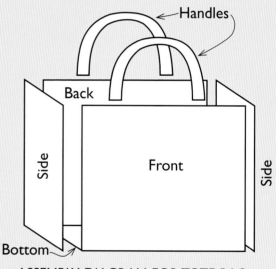

**ASSEMBLY DIAGRAM FOR TOTE BAG**

**4** Assemble lining in the same manner, but trim $1/2$ inch (13mm) from top edges of interfacing before turning top edges of fabric to wrong side. Topstitch along top edge. Insert lining into bag, wrong sides together and seams matching. Pin along top edge.

**5** For handles, fuse batting to center of lining on the wrong side. Fold long edges of each chenille and lining piece $1/2$ inch (6mm) to wrong side and press. Pin chenille handle and lining together with wrong sides facing; topstitch all around. Insert ends of handles between lining and chenille bag, 6 inches (15cm) from side seams. Topstitch through all layers at base of handles. Slipstitch lining in place all around top edge of bag.

# Duffel Bag

**Size:** 21½ inches (55cm) long

## What You'll Need

▶ Chenille bedspread

▶ 1½ yards (1.4m) coordinating fabric, for lining

▶ Sewing thread to match fabrics

▶ 2 yards (2m) fusible batting

▶ One 16-inch (41cm) zipper in matching color

▶ Pencil; compass; yardstick; dressmaker's marking pencil

▶ Sewing machine with zipper foot attachment

## What To Do

1 From chenille bedspread and lining cut the following pieces, which include ½-inch (13mm) seam allowance: First, cut a 22½ x 32½-inch (57 x 82.5cm) rectangle for body of duffel; also cut 2 circles 10½ inches (27cm) in diameter for ends of duffel and 2 rectangles 3 x 17½ inches (7.5 x 44.5cm) for handles. Cut fusible batting ½ inch (13mm) smaller all around for each piece. Center and fuse batting to wrong side of lining pieces.

2 To stitch, use ½ inch (13mm) seam allowances throughout. Fold chenille body fabric crosswise in half with right side in. Pin and stitch for only 3 inches (8cm) from both sides to form cylinder and leave opening for zipper. Press seam allowances open, and press edges in between ½ inch (13mm) to wrong side.

3 Center zipper between seamed areas, pin, and then baste folded edges ¼ inch (6mm) from zipper teeth. Baste zipper to one side, then to the other and test zipper for alignment. Using a zipper foot, machine-stitch along one side, open zipper, then stitch along other side.

4 Pin a chenille circle at either end of chenille cylinder and stitch in place, easing as needed. Clip into seam allowances along

curves. Stitch lining pieces together in the same way but omit zipper. Open zipper and insert lining into bag with wrong sides facing. Working from the inside, slipstitch lining along zipper.

5 Make handles in same manner as Tote Bag on page 44. Turn ends 1 inch (2.5cm) to wrong side and pin. Pin ends of one handle to one side of bag, 2 inches (5cm) from zipper, handle ends 3½ inches (9cm) apart, and centered on side. Topstitch across handle to secure in place ⅜ inch (1cm) from folded end and then again 1¼ inch (3.2cm) from folded end of handle. Repeat on other side of duffel.

# Toddler-Size Jacket

**Size:** Toddler's sizes 2–4

## What You'll Need

▶ Crib- or twin-size chenille bedspread

▶ 1½ yards (1.4m) printed cotton fabric, for lining

▶ Sewing thread to match fabrics

▶ Small shank-type button

▶ Scrap of narrow elastic, for button loop

▶ Pencil; large sheets of tracing paper

## What To Do

1 Enlarge patterns to full size and trace a separate pattern for front and back. Complete half patterns for back and sleeve as follows: Fold tracing paper in half, lay the long dash lines of each pattern on the fold, trace the pattern, cut it out, and unfold the complete pattern. Patterns include ⅜-inch (1cm) seam allowances.

2 Arrange pattern pieces on chenille bedspread for 1 back; 2 fronts, reversing the pattern to cut a left and right front; and 2 sleeves. Position pieces to make good use of tufted designs. For

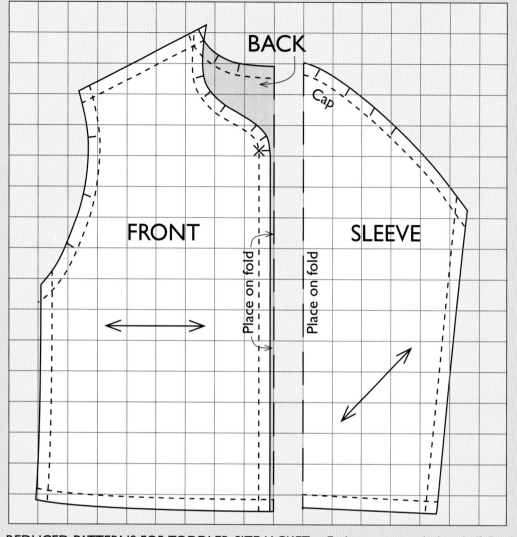

REDUCED PATTERNS FOR TODDLER-SIZE JACKET    Each square equals 1 inch (2.5cm)

example, you may wish to position motifs at center of pieces. Double-ended arrows on patterns suggest a good direction for tufted design lines in the chenille. On our jacket, the bottom edge front and back echoes a scalloped line in the fabric, modifying the straight hem on pattern. When you are pleased with arrangement, cut out pieces. For each chenille piece, cut a same-size lining piece from cotton print fabric.

3 Assemble chenille pieces with right sides facing and corresponding edges even. Stitch, leaving 3/8-inch (1cm) seam allowances. First, pin and stitch fronts to back at shoulder edges. Pin each sleeve to armhole edges of front and back, matching center of sleeve cap (highest point of arch) to shoulder seam, and stitch. With right sides in, fold sleeves from cap to hem and align raw edges as well as side edges of front and back. Stitch along these edges in a continuous seam. Assemble lining in the same way.

4 For button loop, cut a 2-inch (5cm) length of narrow elastic. Fold in half and pin ends to one jacket front where indicated by X on pattern. Make sure ends are even with raw edge of jacket and loop faces armhole. Stitch ends close to jacket edge.

5 Pin lining to jacket with right sides facing and seams matching. Stitch all around, leaving neckline and cuff edges open. Clip curves, and turn to right side through the neckline opening. Turn open edges at neckline and cuff 1/4 inch (6mm) to the inside, pin, and baste. Finish neckline with zigzag stitches or slipstitches. Topstitch cuffs and fold up as needed to fit. Sew button to correspond with loop.

# Shower Curtain & Valance

**Sizes:** As shown, **Shower Curtain**, 76 x 66 inches (193 x 168cm); **Valance**, 62 x 18 inches (157.5 x 46cm)

## What You'll Need

▶ Full-size chenille bedspread
▶ Sewing thread to match
▶ Seam binding in same color as bedspread
▶ Grommet fastener, or kit, and 12 large grommets

## What To Do

### SHOWER CURTAIN

1 Measure shower curtain rod for minimum width of curtain, and measure from rod to floor—or at least well past top of bathtub—for desired finished length. As bedspread may be wider and fuller than minimum width needed to cover, strive to use its entire width in order to have finished edges at sides. If cutting bedspread, allow 2 inches (5cm) for side hems, and 4 inches (10cm) for top and bottom hems. Mark and cut bedspread.

2 To hem edges, stitch seam binding to all cut edges. Turn all bound edges to wrong side: Turn side edges 1 inch (2.5cm), top and bottom edges 2 inches (5cm). Stitch in place.

3 Following manufacturer's instructions, apply grommets ³/₄ inch (2cm) from top edge and evenly spaced across curtain. Mount with hooks and liner.

### VALANCE

1 From remaining or coordinating chenille fabric, cut a rectangle 2 inches (5cm) longer than twice the width of curtain rod, if possible, and 4 inches (10cm) longer than desired length of finished valance.

2 Hem edges in same manner as for shower curtain. Insert rod through casing formed at top.

# Lamp Shade

**Size:** 7¹/₂ inches (19cm) high, 10 inches (25.5cm) in diameter at widest point

## What You'll Need

▶ Fabric from a chenille bedspread—we used remnants from the Baby Quilt Set, page 42.
▶ White paper lamp shade to fit lamp
▶ 1 yard (1m) old or new ball fringe, for trim
▶ Pencil; paper; tape for pattern
▶ Spray adhesive
▶ Fabric glue
▶ Glue gun and hot-melt glue stick

## What To Do

1 To make a paper pattern for lamp shade, wrap paper (brown wrapping paper or tissue) tautly around lamp shade until you have a smooth fit. Tape in place. If it's been necessary to gather paper to fit, tape gathers to hold. Fold paper edges to inside of shade at top and bottom edges. Cut paper on the vertical and open. Trim along top and bottom folded lines.

2 Pin pattern to chenille fabric, centering a motif, if possible. Cut fabric ¹/₂ inch (13mm) larger than pattern all around. Spray adhesive on wrong side of fabric. Let set for a few minutes until tacky to the touch. Wrap fabric around lamp shade, allowing ¹/₂ inch (13mm) to extend at top and bottom. Fold the overlapping vertical edge to wrong side and secure with fabric glue. Bring extending edges at top and bottom to inside surfaces and press to adhere. Clip fabric to accommodate bulb clamp or other support hardware.

3 To add an appliqué, see Step 1 of Heart Pillow in Baby Quilt Set on page 42. If a contrast-color stripe is available on chenille remnants, cut it to the circumference of shade at top, leaving a ¹/₂-inch (13mm) margin of fabric to either side of stripe. Fold along stripe, and hot-glue neatly around top rim, with margins glued to inside surfaces of lamp. Hot-glue ball fringe to bottom rim, with pompons extending past edge and ends overlapping neatly.

# $\mathcal{Q}$uilts

Antique quilts should never be cut up! They're a tangible connection with previous generations, pieces of our history. However, their tattered, stained, and fragmented younger sisters are worth a second look. Individual blocks, unfinished and remnant quilts are handmade "fabric" that is perfect for creating your own easy-to-make heirlooms.

Create your own wall quilt by collecting individual quilt blocks and mounting them on Styrofoam squares. Choose matching blocks, a favorite pattern or color scheme, or one each of several designs. The rag doll is made out of a quilt fragment.

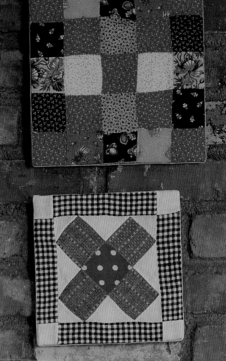

As a quilt-lover and serious collector, there's no way that I would ever suggest that someone cut up any quilt in salvageable condition. It would be a sacrilege, not to mention an extravagance. However, you're not likely to come across many well-preserved, reasonably priced quilts at flea markets, yard sales, or thrift shops (usually the dealers have been there first). If you do happen to find a bargain, fresh from someone's attic, and it's love at first sight, grab it and treasure it. What you're more likely to find will be a variety of damaged quilts and quilt remnants. This is a good opportunity to rescue these orphaned quilts, which are usually quite affordable. Perhaps they're affordable because no one knows what to do with them. This chapter will suggest a number of options.

### A LITTLE HISTORY

In 18th-century America, pioneer women stitched quilts to keep their families warm. The fabrics used were often scraps of worn garments and household linens carefully saved and traded. Pieces of aprons and shirts, petticoats, and children's clothing, lovingly stitched together by candlelight, chronicled lives. These necessary bedcovers, one of the few creative outlets for women in earlier times, are now considered an important contribution to American folk art.

It is through these generations of quilts that we can view our heritage. Differing lifestyles in various regions of the country influenced the style of the quilts. In the colder Northeast, where people wore heavier clothes and winters were harsh, sturdier fabrics and subdued colors were used. In Southern climates, more delicate fabrics made their way into quilt tops along with finer stitches; after all, it was easier to stitch through fine linen and silk than through flannel and wool. Probably the greatest number of quilts were made in America during the 19th century. Patterns began to appear in *Godey's Lady's Book* and newly bought textiles found their way into quilts.

Quilts are basically comprised of three layers. The *quilt top* is the decorative layer. A quilt top can be "pieced," which means that many small pieces (or patches) of fabric are joined together usually in geometric patterns. Or a quilt top can be "appliquéd," which means that small pieces of fabric have been cut into shapes and then layered and stitched onto larger pieces of fabric to form a design. The middle layer is the *batting.* Originally hand-carded cotton or homespun wool, most 20th-century quilts have commercial cotton or—by the 70s—polyester batting. The bottom layer, or *backing,* can be a single sheet of fabric or several strips sewn together.

These three layers are joined together with quilting stitches, which create patterns of their own. Early stitching patterns relied on yardsticks to mark straight lines for boxes, diagonals, or grids and on household objects such as a teacup or pocket watch for curved lines. More intricate stitching patterns were exchanged among friends and relatives. By the end of the 19th century, patterns and perforated templates for stitching designs could be purchased. Quilt patterns were available as well. Newspapers published designs on a weekly basis. And by the 1920s and 1930s preprinted quilt patterns (and even kits complete with fabrics) were advertised in magazines including *Good Housekeeping, McCall's,* and *Ladies' Home Journal.* These kits could be purchased with 12 blocks

**This quilt section was just the right size for a handsome collar. It's an attractive accessory to wear over a solid-color dress or sweater.**

Our patchwork teddy is a toy that even grown-ups will love.
The whimsical rabbit, borrowed from a Texas friend, Jean
Wilkinson, usually resides on a living room chair. Imagine a
bevy of these bunnies along the back of a sofa.

A quilt top purchased for $28 provided more than enough fabric for these two duffel bags. I think that this anonymous 1950s stitcher would be pleased to know that the quilt top she never finished was put to good use after all.

for a child's bed, or 32 for a full-size bed. Pattern choices kept up with technology: In the 1920s and 1930s, cars and planes were in demand and by the 1960s, there were rocket ships. Many of us can still remember our mothers and grandmothers stitching appliqué quilt tops ordered by mail in the 1950s.

Most of the quilts purchased for use in this chapter are from the 1930s through the 1950s. These are the quilts that you're likely to find at flea markets today.

## SHOPPING FOR DAMAGED QUILTS

You will come across tattered quilts that are stained or otherwise damaged beyond repair and most people will simply pass them over. These are referred to as "cutter" quilts. They have suffered from the wear and tear of daily use and years of laundering, exposure to the sun, or mildew or moth damage. Perhaps they were Linus-style "security blankets" once loved by an adorable three-year-old but now outgrown. Maybe a new puppy chewed a hole right in the middle or someone left ink stains while writing in bed. As a result of improper storage some quilts may have serious, discolored crease lines that are permanent and disfiguring.

However, these are exactly the quilts that deserve a second look as there could well be unblemished sections large enough to lend themselves to a stunning jacket or to adorable toys such as our Patchwork Teddy and Rabbit. And, you'll be starting out with handcrafted fabric. It's difficult to be specific about prices for damaged quilts as each one is different and it's also a matter of personal taste. The general range is anywhere from $40 to $100. I purchased a yellow "Wedding Ring" quilt in Amarillo, Texas, that had a number of holes from cigarette burns for $55; there were enough good sections to make the teddy bear, 4 place mats, and still have enough left over for other projects.

## QUILT BLOCKS

Look for individual quilt blocks, sometimes pinned together in groups of four or six or maybe more. Someone had the best intentions of making a quilt but never quite got past the first dozen squares. Usually, these will be pieced cotton (maybe wool) without any batting or backing. The prices can vary from $2 to $12 per square, depending on the age and condition of the fabrics, the intricacy of the pattern, and the workmanship. It's a good bet that if you offer to buy the whole batch, the price will come down. Single squares, with pleasing graphics, can be interesting decorating accessories simply framed and displayed on a wall. But don't hesitate to stitch a group together for a small throw or wall hanging. It doesn't matter if they

Start a family tradition with these one-of-a-kind Christmas stockings made from sections of quilts or quilt tops. It's a chance to pass on a little piece of history. The medium-size stocking (top) is made from a "yo-yo" quilt top remnant which is made of shirred circles of calico fabric with open centers.

match as long as there is some design element that unifies them: for example, all geometrics, different versions of a single pattern (all log cabin variations), the same color combinations, all appliquéd children's subjects; similar prints, or simply the same-scale squares.

## QUILT TOPS

Another worthwhile category for shoppers is quilt tops. Considerably less expensive than finished quilts, they are made up of joined quilt squares but have not been sewn together with batting or backing or binding and there are no quilting stitches holding layers together. These tops can often be spotted at quilt shows but the prices there may be slightly higher as these events draw an attendance of dedicated quilters

who are willing and able to complete these finds and restore them to the purposes for which they were originally intended. However, when you do discover these tops at flea markets or your neighbor's garage sale, take time to consider the possibilities. Some homeowners showcase them at windows by adding a lining and draping them, as a swag, over a curtain rod or dowel. Especially appealing in Early American homes, this window treatment is gaining ground in contemporary homes as well. The quilt top used for the duffel bags on page 52 is particularly interesting. The quilter used newspapers as templates for her pattern pieces—often the pages from television listings. By noting the shows listed, including *Ed Sullivan*, *Voice of Firestone*, *Alcoa Theater,* and *Your Hit Parade* (and the names of the scheduled guests), we were able to estimate the age of the quilt by contacting the Museum of Television and Radio in New York City. They verified that the newspapers were published from 1953 to 1962.

## CRAZY QUILT FRAGMENTS

Crazy quilts were made in Victorian times as "show quilts" and were seldom intended to be used on beds. For this reason, fragile silks and velvets were used in their construction. Quiltmakers of this period excelled in ornamentation and decorative stitching. Irregularly shaped fabric pieces are joined together with intricate embroidery. It's not at all unusual to find hand-painted sections, stuffed flowers and/or grapes, appliqués and laces, wonderful commemorative ribbons documenting political events (look for ones with dates), and even sections of beading. Because these quilts were made from fragile fabrics, the years have not always been kind to them. Therefore, you may well find fragments of crazy quilts that have beautiful detailing—often the quilter's initials and a date will be stitched in a corner. These prized pieces can be used to cover a footstool or to make an eyeglass case or an album cover.

**All it takes is a small section of a special quilt to make up this inviting door knob hanger. Personalize by embroidering your own initials and the date in a corner.**

Quilt blocks and remnants of all sizes and
shapes are perfect for pillows. Try making them
reversible with additional patchwork sections
on the backs.  However, you can also stitch one
or more small pieces onto the front of a ready-
made pillow.

This stunning window treatment was achieved with a colorful quilt top and a fusible window shade. You simply iron the quilt top in place. In this case, there was enough fabric left over to make a matching balloon valance. The quilt pattern is "Grandmother's Flower Garden."

## ODDS AND ENDS

Finally, you will occasionally come across odd shapes that (alas!) someone else has already cut up. These may easily become a table runner, bureau scarf, Christmas ornament, or a pillow top.

## TIPS TO REMEMBER

When buying quilts or sections of quilts, examine the strength of the piece as it relates to the project that you are planning to make. For example, a hand-stitched top—with many small pieces—may pull apart at the seams and not be the best choice for a project that will be handled a lot. Nor is it suitable for a project that will require cutting it up into additional small pieces. A machine-stitched top is sturdier. In any case, it is a good idea to secure a patchwork top with a fusible backing. This will provide extra body, make it easier to work with, and hold the pieces together. Examine both sides of a quilt that you are thinking of buying. Sometimes a stain on the front will not have bled through, so if the quilt has an interesting backing fabric or stitching pattern, you might be able to use that side. Use the quilt design to the best advantage for your project. Cut out pattern pieces from tracing paper and position them on the quilt fabric. Tracing paper is easy to see through and, therefore, allows you to see where the patchwork design fits before you cut into the fabric.

One of the best places to look for old quilts may be in your own attic. A child's quilt that is too worn to be used on a crib again might easily be made into a Christmas stocking for example. There is something very special about handling quilts. Take a moment to think of the original quiltmaker and how satisfying it is to be able to appreciate her creation and yet have the experience of transforming it into something that your own family will now be able to enjoy for generations to come.

This angelic tree ornament is made from a small quilt scrap. All you do is cut out the shape and dip it into fabric stiffener. It's a great holiday gift. Make it an annual event and create a new one each year.

Set a pretty table in a country-style home with pastel patchwork place mats. Leftover cuttings can be fashioned into napkin rings.

# Mounted Quilt Blocks

## Assorted Sizes: Ranging from 8 inches (20cm) square to 16 (41cm) inches square, and one 9$\frac{1}{4}$ x 18$\frac{1}{2}$-inch (23.5 x 47cm) rectangle

## What You'll Need

▶ Quilt blocks or combinations of blocks
▶ Sheets of Styrofoam® plastic foam, $\frac{1}{2}$ inch (13mm) thick
▶ Muslin fabric, for backing
▶ Grosgrain ribbon, $\frac{3}{8}$-inch (1cm) wide
▶ Glue stick, with a temporary bond, for securing fabric to foam
▶ Thick tacky glue, for securing nails to foam
▶ Sawtooth picture hanger with 2 small nails
▶ Ruler or yardstick
▶ Serrated knife
▶ Candle stub or paraffin
▶ Fine-line felt-tip marker; pencil
▶ Pins
▶ Steam iron

## What To Do

1 Press fabrics. Cut muslin to same size as quilt block. Measure quilt block to determine the size of plastic foam backing. Plastic foam should be $\frac{1}{4}$ to $\frac{1}{2}$ inch (6mm-13mm) smaller than fabric to allow any existing seam allowances to fold over edges. Use felt-tip pen and ruler to mark measurements on plastic foam sheet.

2 Wax the knife using a candle stub or paraffin. With a sawing motion, cut out the marked shape from plastic foam for a foundation slab.

3 Use the glue stick to adhere fabric to Styrofoam: With a temporary bond, you can remove the quilt block later and use it for another purpose. Begin by centering the muslin on the foam

block; pin in place. Adhere muslin edges to the edges of the foam slab. Pin to secure until glue bonds. Repeat with quilt block on other side of foam; glue any seam allowances to edges of slab. With the glue stick, apply ribbon around edges, overlapping ribbon ends.

4 Apply hanger to the back of the mounted block, 1 inch (2.5cm) from the top and centered. Dip nails in thick tacky glue and press them through holes in the hanger and muslin into the plastic foam.

# Rag Doll

## Size: 20 inches (51cm) tall

## What You'll Need

▶ Section of patchwork quilt top, about 24 square inches (61cm)
▶ Sewing thread to match
▶ Fusible batting
▶ Polyester fiberfill for stuffing
▶ Needle

## What To Do

1 This doll is similar to the Pillowcase Dolls (see directions beginning on page 22). Here, the legs are finished and positioned slightly differently. Enlarge the patterns for the head/body and leg on page 23 to full size and cut out. Complete the half pattern for the head/body by tracing onto tracing paper folded in half, placing the long dash lines along the fold. Cut out the pattern. Fuse batting to the wrong side of the quilt top, to prevent patchwork seams from opening when the pieces are cut out.

2 Arrange patterns on patchwork. Pin in place, and cut out 2 head/body pieces (for front and back) and 2 leg pieces. Then, reverse the leg pattern, and cut out 2 more leg pieces that are mirror images of the first two.

3 Pin doll pieces together in matching pairs, with right sides facing. Sew $\frac{1}{4}$ inch (6mm) from edges, leaving body and legs open between O marks as indicated on patterns. Clip into the seam allowances as indicated on patterns, and turn pieces to right side. Stuff firmly with fiberfill. For legs, ignore reference to knee joints on pattern, and stuff to within 1 inch (2.5cm) of open edge. Turn bottom edge of body $\frac{1}{4}$ inch (6mm) to inside and insert tops of legs with seams at the sides and feet splayed out. Slipstitch across, closing the opening and securing the legs in place.

# Quilted Collar

## Size: 14 inches (36cm) across and 7 inches (18cm) deep in front and in back

## What You'll Need

▶ Section of quilt, about 18 inches (46cm) square
▶ Same-size piece of muslin, for lining
▶ Approximately 2 yards (2m) preruffled lace trim, 2 inches (5cm) wide
▶ 1 yard (1m) satin ribbon, ³/₈-inch (1cm) wide, for ties at back
▶ Sewing thread to match

## What To Do

1 Enlarge pattern and cut along dash lines for left side back of collar. Cut lining piece to match. Reverse the pattern to cut mirror image for right side and cut another lining piece to match. For front, fold tracing paper in half and trace pattern with long dash lines along the fold. Cut out and unfold pattern. Use this to cut 1 front piece and 1 matching lining piece.

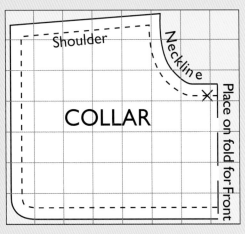

**REDUCED PATTERN FOR COLLAR**
Each square equals 1 inch (2.5cm)

2 To assemble, pin pieces together with right sides facing. Begin by stitching quilted backs to front at shoulders, leaving a ³/₈-inch (1cm) seam allowance. Repeat for lining on one side, but merely baste the other.

3 To add lace trim, pin trim around all but neckline of quilted collar, with right sides facing and edges even. Stitch ¹/₄ inch (6mm) from edges. For ties, cut ribbon in half and pin one end to each side of back where indicated on pattern by an **X**. Pin it to the center of collar back so it does not get caught in stitching.

4 Pin quilted collar to lining, right sides facing and edges even. Stitch all around edges, leaving ³/₈-inch (1cm) seam allowances. Clip into seam allowances along curves and across angles. Open basting stitches in one shoulder of lining and turn collar to right side. Slipstitch opening closed.

# Patchwork Teddy Bear

## Size: 21 inches (54cm) tall

## What You'll Need

▶ Section of a patchwork quilt, approximately 1 square yard (1m)
▶ Sewing thread to match
▶ Polyester fiberfill for stuffing
▶ Scrap of blue felt, for nose
▶ 2 buttons, ⁵/₈ inch (15mm) in diameter, for eyes
▶ Small amount of six-strand embroidery floss, for mouth
▶ 1 yard (1m) ribbon 1⁵/₈ inch (4cm) wide
▶ Tracing paper

## What To Do

1 Enlarge patterns to full size and cut out. You'll need an additional pattern for the back leg/rump section. To create it, fold tracing paper in half, and trace a separate pattern for rump/leg back piece with the long dash lines on the fold; cut out. All patterns include ¹/₄-inch (6mm) seam allowances. Pin patterns to patchwork, reversing the pattern pieces to create a mirror image for the second and fourth pieces. Cut out 2 head fronts, 2 head backs, 4 ears, 2 body fronts, 2 upper body backs, and 1 rump/leg back.

2 To assemble, pin pieces together in matching pairs with right sides facing. Sew with ¹/₄-inch (6mm) seam allowances and leave areas open between **O** marks. Clip into seam allowances as indicated on patterns. Turn pieces to right side. Construct bear as follows.

3 Begin with the head and sew the head fronts together from points A to B, then sew the head backs together from A to C. Pin the joined head front and head back together; stitch around from D to A to D on the other side, leaving the neck edge unstitched.

4 For the body, pin, then sew the body fronts together from points B to E. Pin, then sew the upper body backs together from C to F, leaving open between **O** marks for turning. Sew the joined body back to the rump/leg back piece along the G-F-G edge. Pin the joined body front to the joined body back. Stitch all around the shoulders, arms, sides, and legs, but leave open at the neck.

**5** Attach the head to the body: Pin neck edges together with right sides facing, matching Bs in front, Cs in back, and side seams. Stitch. Clip along all curves as designated on pattern. Turn to right side through the opening that was left at center of upper body back.

**6** Stuff teddy bear with fiberfill. Turn in open edges at back and slipstitch closed.

**7** Sew the ears together in pairs, leaving the slightly curved bottom edge unstitched. Clip and turn; do not stuff. Turn bottom edges 1/4 inch (6mm) to inside, and pinch a small pleat at the center of this edge to cup the ear slightly. Slipstitch edge closed, and pin to bear's head with H and J points matching and with concave side facing front. Slipstitch ears in place.

**8** For face, refer to photograph and make features as follows: For nose, cut an isosceles triangle with 1 inch (2.5cm) sides from felt. Glue to center of front seam. For eyes, stitch a button above each top corner of nose. For mouth, use embroidery floss to form an inverted "Y" with 3 long straight stitches. (For very young children, you may wish to embroider eyes and nose as well.) Tie a bow around the neck.

## Patchwork Rabbit

**Size:** Approximately 14 inches (35.5cm) long

### What You'll Need

▶ Section of patchwork quilt, 14 x 17 inches (35.5 x 43cm)

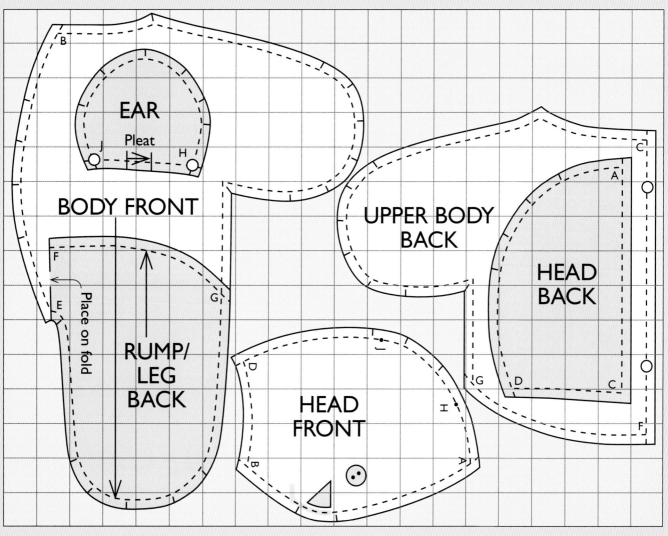

**REDUCED PATTERNS FOR PATCHWORK TEDDY BEAR**          Each square equals 1 inch (2.5cm)

- Same-size piece of muslin fabric or quilt, for backing
- Sewing thread to match
- Polyester fiberfill for stuffing
- 2 pink $^1/_2$-inch (13mm) sew-through buttons

## What To Do

1 Enlarge pattern to full size and cut out. Arrange pattern on quilt section. Pin pattern in place and cut out 1 piece for front. Pattern includes $^1/_4$-inch (6mm) seam allowances. Cut a same-size back from muslin or quilt.

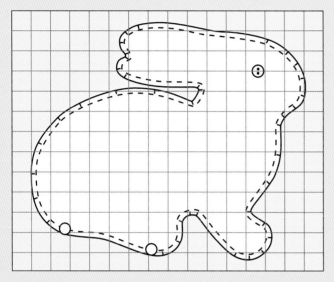

**REDUCED PATTERN FOR PATCHWORK RABBIT**
Each square equals 1 inch (2.5cm)

2 Pin front and back pieces together with right sides facing. Sew all around, leaving $^1/_4$-inch (6mm) seam allowances and leaving areas unstitched between **O** marks as shown on pattern. Clip into seam allowances as indicated on pattern. Turn to right side.

3 Stuff rabbit with fiberfill. Turn in open edges and slipstitch closed. For eyes, stitch a button to either side of face where indicated. For young children, substitute embroidered eyes for buttons.

## Duffel Bags

**Sizes: Large,** 21$^1/_2$ inches (55cm) long
**Small,** 16 inches (41cm) long

### What You'll Need

- Sections from a patchwork quilt or quilt top—we made both from a twin-size top

- Coordinating solid-colored fabric, for lining and straps: 1$^1/_2$ yards (1.4m) for large duffel, 1 yard (1m) for small duffel
- Navy piping: 7 yards (7m), for large duffel; 5$^1/_4$ yards (5m), for small duffel
- Sewing thread to match fabrics and piping
- Fusible batting: 2 yards (2m), for each duffel
- Navy zipper: 22-inch (56cm), for large duffel; 16-inch (41cm), for small duffel
- 3 yards (3m) seam binding, for turning straps
- Pencil; compass; yardstick; dressmaker's marking pencil
- Sewing machine with zipper foot attachment

### What To Do

1 Cut the following circles and large rectangles from both quilt top and lining fabric. These dimensions include $^1/_4$-inch (6mm) seam allowances: For the large duffel, cut a 22 x 32-inch (56 x 82cm) rectangle for body of duffel and 2 circles, 10 inches (25.5cm) in diameter, for ends. For the small duffel, cut a 17 x 23-inch (43 x 58.5cm) rectangle for body of duffel and cut 2 circles, 8$^1/_2$ inches (22cm) in diameter, for ends. Cut fusible batting $^1/_4$ inch (6mm) smaller all around for each piece. Center and fuse batting to wrong side of cut quilt pieces.

2 Apply piping around each circular end, referring to the section on trimming how-to's in the General Directions, Chapter Eight.

3 To make the strap/handle ring, cut 2 long strips from solid-color fabric, piecing as necessary to obtain the required length: For large duffel, cut each 2$^1/_2$ x 90 inches (6.5 x 229cm); for small duffel, 1$^5/_8$ x 69 inches (4 x 175cm). Cut 1 strip of fusible batting $^1/_2$ inch (13mm) narrower than fabric strip. Fuse batting to

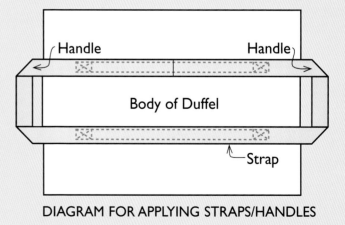

**DIAGRAM FOR APPLYING STRAPS/HANDLES**

one of the strips along center of wrong side. Apply piping to long edges of other strip. Place piped strip and batting-backed strip together with right sides facing and edges even. Insert seam binding in between, running lengthwise along the center and extending slightly at one end, and pin together. Use zipper foot to stitch strap pieces together along previous lines for piping. Also stitch seam binding to one of the ends. To turn strap to right side, pull on seam binding at free end until strap is right side out. Cut stitching to remove seam binding. Press strap. Fold strap crosswise in half, bringing short ends together. Stitch across short ends, ¼ inch (6mm) from raw edges, to form a ring.

Arrange and pin strap ring on duffel bag rectangle as shown in the diagram on page 61. Straps should be centered and 6 inches (15cm) apart. Use a zipper foot to topstitch as indicated by dotted line on diagram, stopping 3 to 4 inches (7.5 to 10cm) from shorter edges of quilt top rectangle to leave handles free. Reinforce ends of stitching as shown on diagram.

**4** To assemble body of duffel, refer to Steps 2 through 4 of Duffel Bag on page 45 in Chenille chapter. Pin handles out of the way to ensure that they don't get caught in stitching.

# Christmas Stockings

**Sizes: Large**, 18 inches (46cm); **Medium** (yo-yo), 15 inches (38cm); **Small**, 8 inches (20.5cm)

## What You'll Need

▶ Section of a quilt or quilt top for front, approximately ⅝ square yard (.6m) for large and medium stockings, 10 square inches (25.5cm) for small stocking
▶ Coordinating fabric or quilt section for back, lining, and background for yo-yo remnant
▶ Matching sewing thread
▶ Fusible batting
▶ Optional trims, such as the lace for cuff on small stocking
▶ Iron and pressing cloth

## What To Do

**1** Enlarge pattern for desired-size stocking. *Solid lines on these patterns represent stitching lines.* Pin patterns to fabrics and add

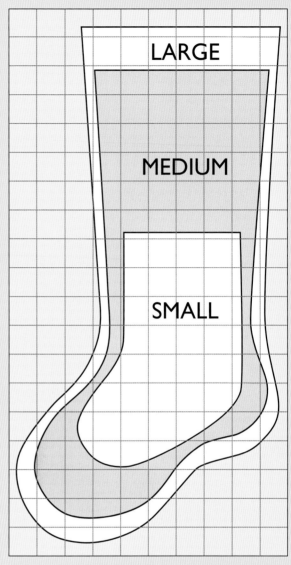

**REDUCED PATTERNS FOR STOCKINGS**
Each square equals 1 inch (2.5cm)

½ inch (13mm) all around for seam allowance. Cut the following pieces, reversing the pattern to cut a mirror image for the back: From quilt section, cut 1 front and 1 back (or use coordinating fabric for back). If using a remnant of a yo-yo top, which has open centers, cut a front from solid fabric to use as a background. Then cut a front and back for lining. Omitting seam allowances, cut 1 piece from fusible batting to match patchwork front or back. (This will give the patchwork body and keep it from coming apart.)

**2** Center batting on wrong side of patchwork piece, and iron to fuse. (For yo-yo stocking, slipstitch remnant to background.) Stitch on any desired trims, such as the lace cuff on the small stocking, at this time.

3 Using $^1/_2$-inch (13mm) seam allowances, pin exterior stocking pieces together with right sides facing and edges even. Sew all around, leaving top edge open. Repeat for lining. Turn stocking right side out. Place lining inside stocking with lining toe fitting inside stocking toe and seams matching. Press, using a pressing cloth. To make a cuff, cut a strip of quilt (or solid-color) fabric 3 inches (7.5cm) deep and the same width as the stocking top plus $^1/_4$ inch (6mm) on each short side for seam allowance. Hem bottom and sides of cuff. Pin cuff in place with top edge inserted $^1/_2$ inch (13mm) between lining and stocking front. Slipstitch around the inside top edge to secure lining top and cuff to stocking top. For a hanging loop, cut a 6-inch (15cm) length of ribbon. Fold crosswise in half and stitch ends securely to inside top of stocking on heel side.

# Door Knob Hanger

**Size:** $4^1/_2$ x $6^1/_2$ inches
(11.5 x 16.5cm)

## What You'll Need
▶ Crazy quilt block, at least 5 x 7 inches (12.5 x 18cm)
▶ Fusible batting
▶ Velvet fabric, 5 x 7 inches (12.5 x 18cm), for backing
▶ $^5/_8$ yard (.6m) twisted cord, for trim
▶ Sewing thread to match twisted cord
▶ Polyester fiberfill, for stuffing
▶ 16-inch (41cm) length of grosgrain ribbon, $^3/_8$-inch (1cm) wide

## What To Do
1 Cut a rectangle 5 x 7 inches (12.5 x 18cm) from a crazy quilt block, from fusible batting, and from velvet. Fuse batting to the wrong side of the crazy quilt rectangle. Pin ends of grosgrain ribbon to the long edge of the crazy quilt rectangle, which will become the top, with each end 1 inch (2.5cm) from a corner. Fold up the ribbon in between and pin it to the center of the rectangle to keep it from getting caught in the stitching.

2 To assemble, pin crazy quilt and velvet rectangle together with right sides facing and edges even. Stitch around $^1/_2$ inch (13mm) from edges, rounding the corners slightly and leaving 3 inches (7.5cm) unstitched along the bottom edge. Clip corners, and turn piece to right side. Stuff plumply. Turn edges to inside and slipstitch opening almost all the way closed. Slipstitch twisted cord all around along the seam, tuck ends into the tiny remaining opening, and stitch it closed.

# Pillows from Quilts

**Sizes:** Assorted squares and rectangles, heart;
9 x 10 inches (23 x 25.5cm)

## What You'll Need
▶ Large quilt blocks or sections from quilts
▶ Fusible batting
▶ Same-size pieces of coordinating fabric, for back and for background fabric when using a piece of a yo-yo top
▶ Sewing thread to match fabrics
▶ Polyester fiberfill or appropriately sized pillow form
▶ Large sheet of tracing paper
▶ Optional: Moss fringe or other trim, enough to fit around pillow
▶ For square and rectangular pillows: dressmaker's marking pencil; clear quilter's ruler or T-square;
▶ For Heart Pillow; compass

## What To Do
1 All of these pillows are knife-edge pillows. Back quilt tops with fusible batting. Refer to the pillow-making section of the General Directions, Chapter Eight. Make a closed pillow, or one with an overlapped back. Refer to the trimming section of the General Directions to add moss fringe or other trim.

2 For Heart Pillow, follow diagram on page 41 to draw a half heart on paper folded in half. Use a compass to draw the half circle at top with a 4-inch (10cm) radius. Unfold paper; if desired, adjust heart shape. Pin pattern to quilt section, positioning as desired. Adding $^1/_2$ inch (13mm) for seam allowances all around, cut out heart shape for pillow top. Repeat for pillow back.

Assemble pillow, following step 2 of Heart Pillow on pages 40-41, but use $^1/_2$-inch (13mm) seams.

# Balloon Valance

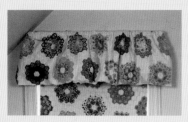

**Size:** To fit

## What You'll Need

▸ Quilt top; we used 1 twin-size top for both valance and window shade
▸ Lightweight fabric for lining
▸ Sewing thread to match fabrics
▸ Curtain rod and hardware

## What To Do

1 Install curtain rod if necessary. Measure rod and cut quilt top 1¹/₂ times this length, to allow for some gathering along the rod, by 26 inches (66cm), which allows for a 1¹/₂-inch (4cm) casing and 10¹/₂-inch (27cm) drop. Cut lining fabric to same size.

2 To make lining, pin quilt top and lining fabric together with right sides facing and edges even. Stitch all around ¹/₄ inch (6mm) from edges, leaving a 5-inch (12.5cm) opening for turning. Clip corners and turn to right side. Turn open edges to inside and machine-stitch opening closed.

3 To create the balloon effect, fold lined fabric lengthwise in half, with quilt top right side in. Pin, then stitch ¹/₂ inch (13mm) from long edges to create a tube. Turn to right side.

4 Determine which part of this newly created tube will be used for the valance front, making sure that the seam is hidden at the top and back. Pin the valance in this arrangement. To make a casing, stitch across 1¹/₂ inches (4cm) from the top. Insert rod through casing and distribute gathers evenly along rod.

# Window Shade

**Size:** To fit

## What You'll Need

▸ Quilt top; we used 1 twin-size top for both valance and window shade
▸ Pellon® Wonder Shade® fusible shade backing
▸ Pellon® Wonder Web® Tape
▸ Size-at-home window shade (for slat and roller)
▸ Duct tape
▸ Steam iron
▸ Pencil; large clear quilter's ruler (square or rectangle) or yardstick and T-square

## What To Do

1 Use small scrap of quilt fabric and fusible shade backing to test adhesion.

2 Measure length of window; add 12 inches (30.5cm) to determine length of shade. To determine width of shade, measure roller to fit window; add 2 inches (5cm). With the yardstick, or a long ruler, and/or a T-square for right corners, mark fusible shade backing to match these measurements. Cut shade. Position the quilt design on the shade, as desired, and cut quilt top to same size.

3 Fuse backing to wrong side of quilt top piece, following manufacturer's instructions for shade backing. A pieced fabric will require some patience. Start at the center and work out, pressing evenly all around

4 Trim shade to exact width of roller. Satin-stitch by machine, using a very close zigzag stitch, around side and bottom edges to finish.

5 To create a slat casing, fold up 1¹/₂ inches (4cm) at bottom edge of shade; press to form a crease. Place slat, trimmed to fit, inside fold. Cut fusible tape to width of shade; place above slat, in hem allowance. Press top edge of hem allowance to fuse. Or, if you prefer, machine-stitch across for slat casing. Attach shade to roller with duct tape.

# Hexagonal Pillow

**Size:** 12 inches (30.5cm) across, not including ruffle

## What You'll Need

▸ Large quilt block or motif, here a Grandmother's Garden motif of hexagonal patches
▸ 2 pieces of coordinating fabric, 1 inch (2.5cm) larger all around than quilt motif
▸ Sewing thread to match fabric
▸ Approximately 1¹/₄ yards (1.25m) preruffled lace trim, 2 inches (5cm) wide

## What To Do

1 Appliqué quilt block to pillow top as follows: Center quilt block right side up on one piece of fabric, pinning it in place. Turn seam allowances along outside edges of block to wrong side, and pin. Slipstitch all around.

2 Add trim and assemble this knife-edge pillow, referring to the trimming how-tos and pillow-making section of the General Directions, Chapter Eight.

## Angel Ornament

**Size:** 5 x 6 inches (12.5 x 15cm)

### What You'll Need

▶ 6 x 7-inch (15 x 18cm) quilt scrap
▶ 1-inch (2.5cm) square of red or pink fabric for heart
▶ 12-inch (30.5cm) length of satin ribbon, $^1/_{16}$-inch (2mm) wide, for hanging loop
▶ Fabric stiffener
▶ White glue
▶ Clear plastic wrap
▶ Yarn or embroidery needle with a sharp point

### What To Do

1 Enlarge patterns for angel and heart on a photo copier by 200%.

2 Place enlarged pattern on quilt scrap. Pin in place and cut out. Use heart pattern to cut 1 heart from pink or red fabric. Use needle to pierce a hole into the top of angel for hanging loop.

3 Place patterns on a work surface and cover with a sheet of clear plastic wrap. Pour fabric stiffener into a bowl and immerse angel cutout, then heart, into stiffener. Make sure fabric is saturated. Run it between your fingers to squeeze out excess stiffener, then place angel and heart on plastic wrap directly over their corresponding patterns. Shape fabrics to conform to patterns, and allow to dry.

4 Use glue to adhere heart to angel, referring to pattern and photograph for position. Let dry. To hang angel, re-pierce hole if necessary, thread ribbon through hole, and tie ends together and make a bow.

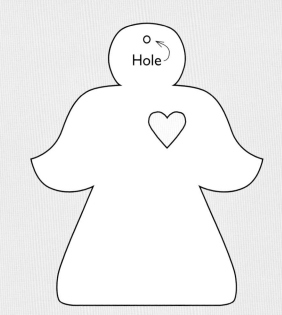

REDUCED PATTERN FOR ANGEL  Enlarge 200%

## Place Mats

**Size:** 13 x 19 inches (33 x 48.5cm)

### What You'll Need For Each

▶ Rectangular section of a quilt, 13 x 19 inches (33 x 48.5cm)
▶ 1$^1/_2$ yards (1.4m) double-fold seam binding
▶ Sewing thread to match seam binding
▶ Optional: dressmaker's marking pencil; round saucer

### What To Do

1 Mark and cut out a 13 x 19-inch (33 x 48.5cm) rectangle from quilt. Round the corners, either freehand or by tracing around a saucer. To make all corners uniform, fold the rectangle in half crosswise, and mark and cut the corners two at a time or else mark one side and then fold in half and match the other.

2 To bind place mat, unfold one edge of seam binding and pin it around place mat, right sides of binding and mat facing and edges even. Stitch in place, along unfolded crease in seam binding. Overlap ends neatly. Turn binding to back of mat and pin in place. Sewing from the right side, topstitch along binding $^1/_8$ inch (3mm) from inside edge to simultaneously secure it to the back.

# Chapter Four

# Lace Trims

At a time when vintage clothing is enjoying renewed popularity, it's not surprising that lacy trims that adorned apparel and household linens are equally appealing. Whether you like hand-crocheted, knit, and tatted edgings or 20th-century machine-made lace, just a few inches can add a touch of romance anywhere in your home.

A dozen elegant, long-stem roses are all made from the same 1950s lace yardage. However, "each blossom could be made from a different lace for a truly mixed bouquet" suggests designer, Betty DeVasto.

Once painstakingly and intricately made to embellish bed linens and bridal gowns or to edge a formal family tablecloth, these gorgeous laces have been removed from their original fabrications. These days, you'll be able to find them at flea markets wound into balls, available by the bagful, or wrapped around cardboard cards and sold by the yard. Here are a number of ways to restore them to a place of honor.

### A LITTLE HISTORY

Lace consists of many strands of thread drawn together to form an intricate, openwork design. From earliest recorded history, lace was an art form, a status symbol, a prized possession. Think of the lace collars and jabots (as in the portraits of Henry VIII), bonnets, parasols, and ball gowns depicted in masterpiece paintings. The more lace, the more prosperous the subject.

I'm using the term "lace" broadly in this chapter as we're not talking about the bolts of lace used for curtains and tablecloths but more about a variety of decorative laces used as trims. However, since the same terms and techniques apply, it's good to have some basic understanding of the subject.

The study of lace is an art in itself and I won't even attempt to describe, in detail, the history or characteristics of the various types of lace. That is better handled by the excellent reference books and catalogs available at museums and libraries. In brief, *needle lace*, which dates back to the 15th century, is considered one of the oldest types of true lace. It consists of rows of looped stitches made, by hand, with a needle and thread. A few examples include the elaborate Alençon, which originated in France in the 17th century, the curvilinear Venetian Gros Point, and smaller-scale Rose Point. A term applied to some of these exquisite laces is "Punto in Aria" or "stitches in the air." Another form of lace-making is *bobbin lace*. For this type, pins attach a pattern to a pillow and then threads, held on bobbins, are woven and braided together to create the lace design. Chantilly is an example of bobbin lace as is Valenciennes, Cluny, and Torchon.

*Machine-made lace* became available at the end of the 19th century and, at the same time, the demand for lace in America grew more widespread. A handbook prepared by the curators of a 1984 exhibition of lace and trims at the Hattiesburg Museum in Mississippi states, "In 1881, Lord & Taylor, in New York City, sold real Valenciennes edging, three inches wide, at $4 to $6 a yard. The machine-made equivalent cost between 40 and 75 cents a yard."

*Crocheted lace* dates back to 16th-century Europe. Originally made in convents, like other forms of needlework, it has been referred to as "nun's lace." Later introduced to Ireland, Irish Rose Crochet is recognizable by tightly-worked three-dimensional floral shapes.

However, you're not going to come across 17th- and 18th-century laces at a neighborhood yard sale; they're safely tucked away in museums. Most of the lacy trims and edgings that you'll find at flea markets were made in America from the 1920s through the 1940s.

Vintage clothing stores, antique shops, and flea markets sell handmade edgings, maybe some bits and pieces of Victorian laces removed from garments and accessories as well as commercially sold 20th-century lace trims.

**These are real eggshells that have been blown out, painted, and then trimmed with scraps of lace. Even the smallest bits and pieces can be used.**

What could be easier, or more effective, than simply lining the shelves of an armoire with delicate lace edgings. It's also a good idea for framing a mantel. Just be sure to have the measurements handy when you shop.

Dress up a plain T-shirt with a crocheted collar or yoke. Once intended as tops for nightgowns and other garments, these delicate pieces are appropriate for many new uses. The butterfly design is an excellent example of filet crochet, and the pink-and-white yoke is an illustration of Irish rose crochet.

## SHOPPING FOR HANDMADE EDGINGS

Most of the edgings that you'll find were made in the 1920s, 1930s, and 1940s, and have been removed from sheets and pillowcases. In those years newspapers, magazines, and thread manufacturers regularly offered patterns for edgings: Sometimes a pattern would be inserted in the spool or printed on the back of the label. Usually $1/2$ inch to 4 inches- wide (13mm to 10cm), crochet and knit edgings are made with continuous designs: Some popular crochet motifs include pineapple, shell, scallops, florals, leaf, lattice, and picot-edge. The majority are white or ecru although there are also some in colors and variegateds.

Like many shoppers, I prefer filet crochet designs, and prices are going up as they become more collectible. Filet crochet, popular in the late 19th and early 20th centuries, requires only two stitches, chain and double crochet, to create a filet (or open) grid and a solid pattern within it. You'll recognize filet crochet by the fact that you can see actual shapes, or words, worked within the stitching. I recently saw a stunning section of filet crochet removed from a 1940s pillowcase that repeated the word "love" in the design; initials and dates can be spotted as well.

Hairpin lace, an airier handmade edging, is also a form of crochet: Threads are wrapped around a hairpin shape, then crocheted in the center and crocheted again later to join the loops into an interesting design.

Tatted lace, made on a small shuttle, is a knotted lace which creates circular, snowflakelike edgings.

The prices of edgings depend on the skill of the needleworker, the condition of the piece, and the intricacy of the design. A matching set from a sheet and pillowcases—in excellent condition, with a unique feature such as the "love" motif mentioned above—could easily demand $100 to $150, or even more. Whereas just a small section might be priced at $10. Sometimes, these edgings will be sold by the ball, comprised of strips in varying lengths and patterns wound together for $20 or $25. Ask to unroll the ball to see that, even if the best sample is on the outside, there are also worthwhile sections inside. Other times, these edgings are sold by the foot or the yard, costing anywhere from $5 to $25.

## COLLARS, CUFFS, AND YOKES

Sought after today as wearable collectibles, these accessories were all the vogue in the early 1900s. They were made as tops for nightgowns, camisoles, chemises, and "corset covers." A 1916 advertisement by Kloster Crochet and Embroidery Cottons, featuring a woman in a nightgown with a crocheted bodice, read: "Real edgings are scarcer and harder to buy so milady makes her own...that is why at every 'crochet klatch' you see so many ladies using Kloster."

A variety of lace trims were dyed (the darker ones remained in the dye bath longer) and then glued around store-bought lamp shades. The effect is very dramatic when the light shows through.

This pair of pillows makes the most of limited amounts of wider laces. Arrange laces patchwork-style or create a woven pattern. Choose a background fabric that accentuates the lace.

Some of the yokes are made with cap sleeves or have a section that fits under the arm and around the bodice; often there will be a place to thread ribbon through the yoke or collar. When thinking about purchasing one of these to be worn, try it on first—sizes were smaller then and some tops have shrunk with use. Most crocheted or knit yokes, such as the ones shown here, range in price from $12 to $25 although you will also see fine examples for $75 to $100.

The yokes or tops, without sleeve portions are more versatile; originally the fabrics held them together at the sides. If you're a patient shopper, they can be found for $20, and even less—but you'll also see them for $45 and $55.

Collars and cuffs can, of course, be used for the purpose for which they were originally intended. Matching sets are not easy to come by: These are often snapped up by dressmakers and designers who make vintage-style clothing. Collars may close at the front, at the back, or come in two pieces—a back and a front. An intricate Irish crochet collar made of fine threads can be $40 to $45 and even more. Less ornate ones will be priced at $25 or less.

**COMMERCIAL LACE**

By commercial lace, I'm referring to the machine-made laces that were popular from the 1920s right through the 1950s. Lace was a fashion necessity and appeared on dresses, lingerie, children's clothes, hats, and even aprons. When these garments wore out, the lace was carefully removed and set aside for future use. Lace was also stocked in department stores wrapped around wooden, cardboard, and—later—plastic bolts and sold by the yard. Many were excellent imitations of handmade edgings. For those who shopped by mail, you could order as much as "20 yds. of laces, including eyelets, for $1.00" from the Wotring Co. in Catasauqua, PA, in 1957.

At flea markets, you want to keep an eye out for laces that are still on the original holder as you will get enough matching yardage, in good condition, for some larger projects. For example, I bought a card of 18 yards of cotton lace that was enough to make our bouquet of long-stem roses, the skirt portion of the angel, and part of the two pillow tops. The entire 18 yards cost $25 and there is still quite a bit left over. The dealer bought these quantities of lace at a garage sale; they were the samples of a retired Sears Roebuck salesman.

Narrower laces can be found on index-size cards and sold by the card, the yard, or sometimes by the ball. Prices range from $2 a yard, depending on the quality and quantity of the lace.

**TIPS TO REMEMBER**

Some of the best buys in laces are assorted bits and pieces sold in lots and by the bagful. These odds and ends are what we used for many of the projects shown in this chapter, including the charming Victorian House wall hanging. Don't overlook a tattered tablecloth or pillowcase that might still have a salvageable edging.

Don't always take lace too seriously. A few elbow "patches" can be a great touch for a tailored blazer, or add a collar to a denim jacket.

The appeal of these vintage whites is not only the age of elegance they suggest but their lasting quality in today's fast-changing society.

**There couldn't be a more ethereal material for making an angel than lace. Her delicate wings are net lace that is stiffened, and even her eyelashes are made from scraps of tatted lace.**

It's not surprising that Shirley Botsford, owner of a Victorian bed-and-breakfast in Beacon, NY, chose this design to display her collection of laces.

# Long-Stem Roses

**Size:** Approximately 21 inches (53cm) long

## What You'll Need

▶ 10 inches (25.5cm) of lace trim 3½ to 4 inches (9 to 10cm) wide for each rose
▶ 16-gauge wire, 18 inches (46cm) long
▶ Dark green floral tape
▶ Small and large artificial rose leaves
▶ White glue

## What To Do

1 To form rose, roll lace, pinching 1 end of lace tightly for about 1½ inches (4cm), and glue to secure. Insert stem wire and continue rolling lace, tightly at 1 edge, for base of rose, and more loosely at the opposite edge, for outer tips of petals. With fingers, dab glue on lace edges at base of rose. When you come to the end, turn the raw or cut edge in toward the center and secure with glue. Use floral tape to wrap base of rose tightly.

2 To stiffen lace, mix 1 teaspoon glue and ½ cup of water together. Quickly dip rose in glue solution, fine-tune shape, stand in a vase, and let dry overnight.

3 When dry, use floral tape to wrap 3 small leaves at base of rose. Continue wrapping tape in a spiral down the stem wire, adding large leaves at random. Curve stem and leaves gracefully.

# Lace Eggs

**Size:** Approximately 2½ inches (6cm)

## What You'll Need

▶ Eggs at room temperature
▶ Scraps of lace
▶ Spray paint
▶ White glue
▶ Sharp straight pin, long floral pin, or hat pin
▶ Toothpicks
▶ Thin wood skewers, found in craft and grocery stores
▶ Small block of floral clay, to hold skewers

## What To Do

1 To prepare eggshells, use a pin and poke a small hole in the pointed end of the egg. Carefully expand hole to about the diameter of a pencil. Make another hole at the broad end of the egg. With a long pin or toothpick, break yolk in egg. Shake the egg gently over a bowl, then blow through the first hole until yoke and white of the egg come out the other end. Some people prefer to use the suction of a turkey baster to empty shell. Rinse shell thoroughly and allow to dry.

2 To paint the eggshells, stand wood skewers in floral clay. Set the eggs on the skewers. (It is better to work with just a couple at a time to allow space around them.) Spray-paint eggshells. Allow to dry and add a second coat.

3 To apply lace, place a fine line of glue on the area of the shell that you wish to cover. Use a toothpick to position lace. Allow each row or layer of lace to dry before adding the next.

4 Cover holes in ends of egg with scraps of lace, or glue small pieces of paper over holes and conceal with paint.

# Shelf Edging

**Size:** To fit

## What You'll Need

▶ Assorted widths and types of lace trim
▶ Iron and spray starch
▶ Hammer and small tacks, or staple gun and staples

## What To Do

1 Measure length of shelf. Cut lace trims 1 inch (2.5cm) longer at each end.

2 Spray-starch and press lace trims, turning ends 1 inch (2.5cm) to wrong side. To attach trim to shelf, staple or gently hammer evenly spaced tacks along a straight edge of the trim.

# Dressed-up T-Shirts

**Sizes:** As desired

## What You'll Need for Each
▶ Crocheted lace collar or yoke
▶ T-shirt
▶ Sewing thread to match collar
▶ Pins and needle
▶ Thick magazine

## What To Do
1 Try on the T-shirt, position the collar or yoke in place, and secure with pins. Remove.

2 Insert magazine into T-shirt to keep it from stretching during sewing—and to keep stitches from going through to the back.

3 Slipstitch collar or yoke in place along neckline. Continue to stitch along remaining edges, or leave edges free.

# Lace-Trimmed Lamp Shades

**Size:** As desired

## What You'll Need
▶ White lamp shade(s)—drum shapes are easier to work with
▶ Vintage lace trims in various widths, long enough to fit around shade
▶ Cold-water dyes—we used pink, blue, and turquoise
▶ Rubber gloves
▶ White glue
▶ Straight pins

## What To Do
1 To dye lace, wear rubber gloves and work in a sink or basin. Follow manufacturer's directions for preparing a dye bath. For a range of hues, leave some lace strips in dye bath longer than others. Rinse laces thoroughly and allow to dry; press flat.

2 To cover lamp shade, wrap with lace trims: Begin at the bottom (use any with scalloped edges for bottom row), keeping just inside rim bindings, and work up, overlapping rows slightly. Vary colors, widths, and textures of lace. You may want to try several arrangements before you determine the one you like best. Pin the lace in place as you work. Join short edges of lace for each row with the vertical seam at the back of the shade. When you are satisfied with the arrangement, test-fit each piece of lace trim, and cut as you go so that ends of lace will overlap by $1/2$ inch (13mm) at back. Apply fine lines of glue around lamp shade. Press lace into glue.

# Patches-of-Lace Pillow

**Size:** 13 x 13 x $2^{1}/2$ inches (33 x 33 x 6.5cm)

## What You'll Need
▶ 4 different types of lace fragments, each 4 x 16 inches (10 x 41cm)
▶ 2 yards (2m) cotton chintz fabric
▶ Sewing thread to match fabric
▶ 3 yards (3m) cotton cording, for piping
▶ 16-inch (41cm) square soft pillow form or box pillow form to fit

## What To Do
1 For the pillow, cut the following from chintz fabric: one 14-inch (36cm) square, for pillow back; one $3^{1}/2$ x 55-inch (9 x 140cm) strip—piecing as necessary, for boxing strip; four 4 x 16-inch (10 x 41cm) strips, for pillow top. From remaining fabric, cut strips on the bias 2 inches (5cm) wide and totaling 3 yards (3m) in length, for piping.

2 For lace design on pillow top, make lace/fabric strips first: Pin a different lace trim, right side up, to right side of each fabric strip. Machine-baste close to edges all around. Lay strips side by side, with lace on top and long edges butting. Alternate colors and textures.

3 Pin the first 2 strips together along 1 long edge only, with right sides facing; sew together with $3/8$-inch (1cm) seam allowances. Join the third and fourth strips in the same way. Press seams open.

4 Next, divide strips into squares: Working from the wrong side, fold and press joined strips in half, crosswise, and in half again, with all creases running perpendicular to the seams. Cut along these creases; you should now have 4 strips, each 4 x 13³/₄ inch (10 x 35cm).

5 Arrange these cut strips side by side to form a varied and interesting checkerboard pattern. For more variety, rip out the seams between 2 of the previously joined strips, alternate the laces, and then restitch strips. When you are pleased with the arrangement, sew all 4 strips together, taking care to match the seams and leaving ³/₈-inch (1cm) seam allowances. You should have a 13³/₄-inch (35cm) square for the pillow top.

6 To make piping, follow the trimming how-to's in the General Directions, Chapter Eight. Apply around pillow top and pillow back.

7 Assemble the box pillow, following the pillow-making section of the General Directions. Since box pillow forms are less widely available, a soft, larger pillow may be inserted to fill and conform to the shape.

## Woven-Lace Pillow

**Size:** 25 x 12 x 2¹/₂ inches (63.5 x 30.5 x 6cm)

### What You'll Need
▶ Lace trims 3- to 4-inches (8 to 10cm) wide, totaling 4 yards (4m)
▶ 3 yards (3m) cotton chintz fabric
▶ Sewing thread to match laces and fabric
▶ Two 16-inch (41cm) square soft pillow forms
▶ Optional: Small amount of polyester fiberfill, for extra stuffing

### What To Do
1 From chintz fabric, cut the following: two 13 x 26-inch (33 x 66cm) rectangles for pillow top and back; one 3¹/₂ x 80-inch (9 x 203cm) strip, piecing as necessary, for boxing strip. From remaining fabric, cut strips on the bias 2 inches (5cm) wide and totaling 4¹/₂ yards (4.5m) in length, for piping.

2 For lace weaving over the pillow top, lay 5 strips of lace, evenly spaced and right side up, on a diagonal (as shown in the photograph) over the right side of 1 fabric rectangle. Lay 3 strips diagonally in the other direction on top; rearrange strips until you are pleased with the balance of tones, textures, and widths. At that time, weave the outermost of the 3 strips under, then over, then under the strips it intersects. Weave the middle strip over, then under, then over the strips it intersects. Pin woven laces in place. Using thread to match lace, machine-sew along long edges of each lace strip to secure.

3 To make piping, follow trimming how-to's in the General Directions, Chapter Eight, and apply it around the pillow top and pillow back.

4 Assemble the box pillow, following the pillow-making section of the General Directions. If rectangular box pillow forms are not available, insert 2 soft, larger pillows to fill and conform to the shape; you may wish to add fiberfill to stuff the corners.

## Lace Angel

**Size:** 11 inches (28cm) tall

### What You'll Need
▶ 12-inch (30.5cm) lace or lace-edged square, for top of gown and sleeves
▶ Assortment of lace trims 2 to 5 inches (5 to 13cm) wide, totaling 1 yard (1m)
▶ ⁵/₈ yard (60cm) lace trim ¹/₂-inch (13mm) wide, for halo and ruffled collar
▶ Assortment of lace medallions and small scraps
▶ 6-inch (15cm) square of cream-colored sheer stretch fabric or nylon stocking, to cover head
▶ Ecru sewing thread
▶ 9-inch (23cm) Styrofoam® plastic foam cone, for body
▶ 2¹/₂-inch (6cm) Styrofoam® plastic foam ball, for head
▶ 2-inch (5cm) square of thin quilt batting
▶ Pink chalk or powder blusher
▶ Fabric stiffener
▶ ¹/₂-inch (13mm) craft pins
▶ Pearl beads, for nose and bodice
▶ Gold-color straight pins to fit pearl beads
▶ 12-inch (30.5cm) length of 24-gauge wire

- White craft glue
- Grapefruit knife or apple corer
- Sewing needle
- Glue gun and glue stick
- Plastic wrap

## What To Do

1 To attach head shape to body, use a knife or apple corer to cut a hole 1 inch (2.5cm) in diameter and $^3/_4$ inch (2cm) deep in Styrofoam ball. Push tip of cone into hole and twist to fit.

2 For head, trim batting piece into a circular shape and glue to front of head, for face. Wrap the stretch fabric around the Styrofoam ball tightly (including batting), and gather the edges at the bottom back of head next to hole. Secure by wrapping gathered fabric firmly with thread, then trim fabric close to thread. Apply hot glue to tip of cone and push ball firmly onto cone. Hold until glue sets.

3 For face, refer to actual-size diagram below. Rub a tiny amount of pink chalk or blusher onto cheeks. From narrow lace trim (this one used a piece of tatting), cut 3 thin semicircle strips for eyelashes and a circle for mouth. Use white glue to adhere in position. Pin a pearl bead between eyes, for nose.

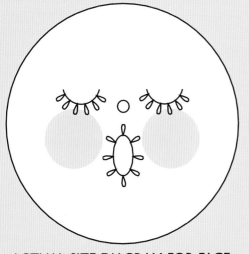

ACTUAL-SIZE DIAGRAM FOR FACE

4 For a cap, gently stretch a strip of lace over head, around face, and pin at the back. Glue small lace motifs or medallions at back and top of head.

5 For a halo, thread thin wire through 1 long edge of a $^1/_2$ x 8 inch (13mm x 20cm) strip of lace. Gather the lace on the wire and bring wire ends together to form a circle 1$^1/_2$ inches

(4cm) in diameter. Twist ends together for $^3/_4$ inch (2cm), to form a stem, then cut away excess. Set halo aside.

6 For wings, cut two 4$^1/_2$ x 10-inch (11 x 25cm) rectangles from fine lace. Use a needle and thread to gather 1 short end of each. Trim the opposite short ends to a curve; see diagram for wing.

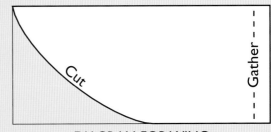

DIAGRAM FOR WING

7 For layered skirt, pin lace around cone 3 inches (7.5cm) from bottom. The lace will bunch at the top edge, so make small gathers evenly around cone and pin to secure. Pin a second strip of lace around cone 5 inches (12.5cm) from bottom. Pin another piece of lace down the back of cone to cover overlapping lace and pin heads.

8 Soak lace—for top of gown and sleeves, the wings, and the halo—in fabric stiffener. Run pieces between your fingers to squeeze out excess fabric stiffener. Spread out laces and blot with a rag to remove stiffener from lace openwork. Spread items on plastic wrap to dry. Place a ball of plastic wrap under gathered ends of wings so they will have a cupped shape near the cone and flare at ends as in photo; distribute gathers evenly on halo. Allow to dry.

9 To create sleeves and top of gown, refer to diagrams below. First, fold 1 long edge of the lace square 1$^1/_2$ inches (4cm) to the right side, and center over front of angel under head. Pin at sides of neck. Fold top corners to center front of cone. Open folded edge somewhat to form rounded sleeves, and insert a bit of wadded up plastic wrap to keep sleeves open while drying.

DIAGRAMS FOR SLEEVES/TOP OF GOWN

10 When lace is dry, remove plastic wrap. Hot-glue wings to back of cone. Glue a lace motif over gathered ends of wings. Glue the ends of the stiffened sleeves together at center front of cone. Push halo "stem" into center of head. Use needle and thread to gather narrow lace for a ruffled collar, and pin to head to secure. Glue a triangular section of lace below collar at center front. Pin pearl beads to lace to secure and embellish.

# Victorian-House Wall Hanging

### Size: 18 x 24 inches (46 x 61cm)

## What You'll Need

▶ Assortment of lace trims:
3 to 4 yards (3 to 4m) of $^1/4$-to $^1/2$-inch (6 to 13mm) widths, 2 to 3 yards (2 to 3m) of $^3/4$-to 1$^1/2$-inch (2 to 4cm), 1 to 2 yards (1 to 2m) of 2- to 3-inch (5 to 8cm) widths, plus patterned lace with medallions, motifs and semicircles that can be cut out

▶ 1 yard (1m) ecru satin ribbon $^1/8$ inch (3mm) wide, for window panes

▶ 2 Styrofoam® plastic foam sheets, 12 x 18 inches x 1 inch deep (31 x 46 x 2.5cm)

▶ $^5/8$ yard (.60m) purple velveteen or felt (Note: Velveteen requires extreme care when steam-pressing lace in place.)

▶ Pellon® Wonder-Under® Transfer Web $^1/2$ yard (.5m) yardage and $^1/4$-inch (6mm) wide Web Tape, to secure lace to fabric

▶ Optional: Purple grosgrain ribbon: 2$^1/2$ yards (2.5m) each $^7/8$ inch (2cm) and 1$^3/8$ inch (3.5cm) wide, for finishing edges

▶ White glue

▶ Round toothpicks

▶ Straight pins

▶ Loose dressmaker's chalk

▶ Steam iron

▶ Staple gun and staples (or convertible stapler)

▶ Picture hangers

## What To Do

1 To make backing, lay Styrofoam sheets side-by-side and join them together along 18-inch (46cm) sides to form one 18 x 24-inch (46 x 61cm) slab; apply white glue along facing edges and insert toothpicks at 2-inch (5cm) intervals through these adjacent edges. Push tightly together, and let glue dry overnight.

2 From fabric, cut a rectangle 2 inches (5cm) larger all around than Styrofoam.

3 Enlarge pattern. To transfer pattern onto velveteen, first use toothpicks to perforate the pattern at each intersection of lines. To transfer design lines, perforate lines of pattern with a pin every $^1/4$ inch (6mm) or so. Center pattern over fabric, and pin to secure. Rub dressmaker's chalk over perforations. Carefully lift pattern away.

4 Plan the placement of trims, using your assortment creatively and referring to the photograph for suggestions. Press all trims beforehand, and cut trims as you go, using a length of trim for each design line, as defined by chalk points. Begin with the narrowest ribbon and trims, then lay on the wider ones. Cover the raw ends of trims by overlapping them with other trims laid over and perpendicular to them. Finally, add the medallions and appliqués at windows, door front, or other areas as shown in photo. Play with the arrangement, and pin or tape pieces together (not to the fabric) in place to temporarily secure.

5 To apply lace to fabric, begin working with the pieces underneath first, then the overlapping pieces. Cover ironing board with a clean cloth to protect it from fusible adhesive. Cut paper-backed web tape to same length as each trim. For wide trims, use tape along all edges. Following manufacturer's instructions, iron web to the back of each ribbon or lace piece. Peel off the paper backing. Position piece, fusible side down, on fabric, and thoroughly steam-press, taking care to keep the iron from touching the velveteen, as it will leave a mark. When the lace is steamed, remove iron and use your fingers to secure it to the pile of the velveteen. When working with long lengths, hold 1 end with a pin and pull the opposite end taut before steaming. Attach medallions and cutouts in the same way as the trims, but use fusible web cut from yardage for these shapes.

Apply a dot of white glue to any area and ends of lace that curl up and might require an extra bond.

6 To mount picture, center the wrong side of the velveteen on the Styrofoam. Use stapler to secure all sides, mitering corners so they are flat. Fold raw edges to the back. If desired, glue the narrower grosgrain ribbon around the outer edge, and cover raw edges on the back with wider ribbon, mitering at corners. Attach picture hangers at center top of back, gluing to secure.

REDUCED PATTERN FOR VICTORIAN HOUSE

Each square equals 1 inch (2.5cm).

Floral-print handkerchiefs are the choice for this attractive wreath: It doesn't matter if they're slightly damaged as only the edges show. Crocheted or other lacy-edge hankies would be equally stunning.

# Chapter Five

# Handkerchiefs

Usually priced under $5, nostalgic 1930s to 1950s handkerchiefs are plentiful. From bold floral prints to delicate crocheted edgings to Valentines, these popular keepsakes offer graphics and handwork for every taste. But once you've collected a drawerful, what can you do to show off your treasures? Read on, to discover many handy ideas for handkerchiefs.

Scalloped floral-print hankies border this tablecloth and additional florals make up the quilted top. Designed in blocks, this same idea could be adapted to a bedcover. Make as many blocks as necessary to fit your table or bed. Note that the rabbit centerpiece is wearing a matching kerchief.

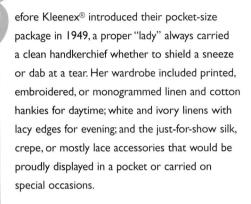

*B*efore Kleenex® introduced their pocket-size package in 1949, a proper "lady" always carried a clean handkerchief whether to shield a sneeze or dab at a tear. Her wardrobe included printed, embroidered, or monogrammed linen and cotton hankies for daytime; white and ivory linens with lacy edges for evening; and the just-for-show silk, crepe, or mostly lace accessories that would be proudly displayed in a pocket or carried on special occasions.

## A LITTLE HISTORY

Early versions of handkerchiefs date back to first-century Rome, when cloth squares were waved to signal applause at gladiatorial competitions. It was Louis XIV who decreed, in 1685, that all handkerchiefs should be square. In the 18th century, when inhaling snuff was in vogue, it was practical for men to carry oversized, 27- to 29-inch (68.5 to 73.5cm), handkerchiefs of the finest fabrics.

*A Hand-book of Etiquette for Ladies,* published in Philadelphia in 1849, reads: "Your handkerchief should be as fine as snowy cobwebs, it should be bordered with deep rich lace and delicately perfumed."

Victorian women carried elaborate silk and lace handkerchiefs lavishly embellished with needlework. Embroideries included mottoes and sentimental sayings. Black or black-edged handkerchiefs were worn during periods of mourning.

According to folklore, lovers exchanged handkerchiefs as a token of betrothal; the gentleman wore his in a hatband or around his arm. It is said that a coquettish woman might "accidentally" drop her handkerchief to attract a suitor's attention—but she never waved it, in public, to attract attention or she would be considered "fast." Even carefully chaperoned young women could communicate with a gentleman using handkerchief signals: Drawing her handkerchief across her cheek conveyed "I love you" and across her forehead meant "We are being watched."

After the turn of the century, handkerchiefs were mass produced in a variety of designs that anyone could afford.

The December 1912 issue of *McCall's Magazine* advertised "Embroidered, Imported Irish Linen Handkerchiefs in a Special Christmas Box" at 3 for 50 cents from The L. H. Field Co., Importers, in Jackson, Michigan. A competitive company in Detroit offered "The finest line of handkerchiefs in America and the best values. Special attention is invited to our choice selections put up in fancy boxes for holiday or birthday gifts;" a box of six different designs could be purchased from them for 75 cents. Although, these were packaged as holiday gifts, in pretty boxes, linen handkerchiefs remained all white. This was not the case with silk handkerchiefs, which were the palest pastels and adorned with delicately detailed embroideries.

**An exquisite wedding handkerchief is transformed into an elegant pincushion. Just the center is backed and padded, and rows of delicate laces form the wide ruffle. This would also be appropriate as a ringbearer's pillow.**

Kleenex® was introduced to the market in 1914, but primarily used as bandages in hospitals during the war, due to the lack of cotton. By 1930, however, advertising was geared toward using disposable tissues instead of handkerchiefs. One newspaper ad campaign in Peoria, Illinois, read "We pay to prove Kleenex® is wonderful for handkerchiefs." The pay was a free box of tissues. Other ads read: "Don't put a cold in your pocket" and "When your girlfriend is crying, don't put a wet handkerchief in your pocket." Sales began to soar. However, there was still the matter of protocol in regard to pulling out a freshly laundered, and delicately patterned, hankie as compared to a crumpled wad of paper.

Reversible handkerchiefs imprinted with intricate maps and codes were distributed to soldiers to be worn around their necks as kerchiefs and used in case of emergency so they could find their way if lost in enemy territory.

By the 1930s, hankies started to be more colorful. Small detailed flowers were printed in overall designs and garlands. Pastels were prevalent, especially pinks and mauves, but there were also subtle reds, browns, and yellows. Backgrounds were usually cream. Edges

were squared off with hand or machine-rolled hems. Some art deco patterns and a few geometric figures also date to the 1930s.

In the 1940s, especially after the war, patterns became bolder, with larger flowers, less detail, and scalloped edges. Colors included stronger pastels along with bright blues, peach, violet, and rose. Backgrounds were still off-white, perhaps with a tone-on-tone line design on them. Handkerchiefs, with large scallops, often measure over 16 inches square (41cm) while the majority of hankies range from 8 to 14 inches (20.5 to 35.5cm).

In the 1950s floral-print handkerchiefs featured bouquets and baskets and—while some of the larger scallops remained—scallops became smaller as the decade continued. Reds, golds, burgundy, purples, turquoise, and yellows were popular, and most of the backgrounds were white. Occasionally, you will find round—floral and holiday-print—handkerchiefs, which had a brief lifespan in the 1950s.

Fellow collector, designer, and author of *Handkerchief Quilts*, Pat Long Gardner favors handkerchiefs by scarf designers from the 1950s. These handkerchiefs bear the designers' signatures. Names to watch for include Tammis Keefe, Peg Thomas, Pat Prichard, Faith Austin, Kati, Billie Kampa, Rutherford, Monique, and Virginia Zito.

Personally, I collect holiday handkerchiefs—especially Valentines. These were manufactured as gift items in the 1950s and were often slipped inside a card and given to a dear friend or relative. Seldom used, these can be found in excellent condition, sometimes with "Made in the Philippines" oval gold labels still in place.

This chapter concentrates mostly on women's handkerchiefs from the 1930s, 1940s, and 1950s. Received as gifts and accumulated by the dozens, they were often tucked away and never used. You'll find that the ways in which you can take advantage of these fabric squares now is nothing to sneeze at.

### SHOPPING FOR FLORAL PRINTS

The most common handkerchiefs that you'll find at flea markets and vintage clothing stores are floral prints. At first glance, they may all look alike.

This sweet little angel's dress is really two Christmas-print hankies with a lace handkerchief for her wings. It's easy to imagine a whole treeful.

Holiday hankies make up these Christmas stockings. The cuff of the poinsettia stocking is an embroidered hankie. Red-and-white crochet (from a hankie, of course) adorns the candy cane design.

Pat Long Gardner designed this quilted holiday hanging around a 1950s Tammis Keefe Christmas hankie, which is used for the center medallion. Handkerchief quilts were popular as far back as the 18th century.

Put your heart on a pillow. Printed cotton and embroidered linen Valentine hankies gaily decorate these "Have-A-Heart" pillows. Pick just one favorite hankie or combine several different ones.

But they're not. Compare the edges, the sizes of the handkerchiefs, and the style and colors of the flowers. Some hankies will have a border of color around the edge and a white center; others will be just the opposite. Flowers may be scattered over the whole surface; a basket or bouquet motif may be stronger in one corner; or there may be a different design in each corner. Think about what you might do with your collection of handkerchiefs and let that influence your choices. For example, you may decide to collect purple florals to make a tablecloth or quilt top. Do you want to limit it to just violets and/or pansies or will any purple flower do? On the other hand, you could seek out as many different examples of purple flowers as possible and simply frame each one, separately, on a guest room wall. Is it important that the edges be scalloped or even? The tablecloth shown on page 82 uses straight-edge hankies for the top and scalloped ones for the edging.

I purchased one 1940s lavender handkerchief that still has an S. S. Kresge Co. price tag on it for 15 cents. Most of the floral-print handkerchiefs today will be priced between $2 and $3. If you're lucky, you'll find some for $1.00.

### FANCY EDGINGS

Patterns for hand-crocheted, tatted, and hairpin lace edgings for hankies were published first in the 1840s, enjoyed a great revival in popularity in the 1940s, and appeared in women's magazines and booklets right up through the 1960s.

An article in the September 1938 *Mother's Home Life and the Household Guest* describes the advantages of handmade crocheted edgings: "We show here examples of the new smart edgings crocheted in lovely colors. These require but small amounts of cotton and add very substantially not only to the beauty but to the value of articles adorned—You probably know what handkerchiefs with handlace edgings cost—yet these shown here are yours at tiny cost and only a short period of easy, fascinating crocheting." A pattern book, advertised in this same issue, could be ordered from Spool Cotton Company in New York City for 10 cents. The American Thread Company published booklets, in 1953, that still

sold for 10 cents and included directions for twenty-six different edgings. These edgings were usually stitched in variegated cotton thread on a white or pastel handkerchief. The handkerchiefs were often worn, with one of the edges folded down, in breast pockets.

I have never paid more than $5 for one of these handkerchiefs but have seen them for as much as $10 or $12. The deeper and more intricate the edging, the higher the cost.

### HOLIDAY HANKIES

Christmas and Valentine's Day handkerchiefs come with printed or machine-embroidered designs: The embroidered hankies are sheerer and smaller, 10 inches square (25.5cm). As I've already mentioned, I collect Valentine hankies and am particularly pleased when I find one with words on it such as "Especially For You" or "Be Mine" or "I Love You." Naturally, most of the Valentine hankies are predominantly red and white. However, if there are rosebuds scattered along the edge, in a nosegay design, a bouquet, or sometimes filling a parasol, the stems and leaves will be green. Other flowers on these handkerchiefs include daisies and forget-me-nots. The color blue appears not only in flowers but also incorporated into borders—perhaps as a ribbon. There are pink hearts, roses, and ribbons, and I have a couple of hankies with pink backgrounds. Other images, in addition to hearts and flowers, may include butterflies, doves, fans, envelopes sealed with a small heart, (often in the beak of a dove)—indicating a love letter, a variety of doily treatments, birdcages filled with hearts and flowers, and angels. One dealer tells me that she is seeing a great demand for Valentine handkerchiefs with cupids and angels, which she thinks date back to the 1940s. "The more cherubs, the better," she says. More often than not, the edges will be scalloped and perhaps reflect a heart shape. Most of these handkerchiefs are at least 12 inches (32.5cm) square. Machine-embroidered Valentine hankies usually have a scattering of tiny red hearts and some white-on-white embroidery.

Embroidered Christmas handkerchiefs feature poinsettias, Christmas ornaments, and candy canes. Printed ones offer more variety: Poinsettias and candy canes remain popular but there are also reindeers, stockings, Santas in sleds, a lot of holly, candles with pine boughs, snowmen (and ladies), snowflakes, bells, and trees. (Bell and tree shapes appear in borders as well.) One of my favorite themes is a Christmas scene of a row of snow-covered houses or a country church, with Santa and his reindeer overhead combined with many of the other holiday symbols.

Most holiday handkerchiefs can be found for no more than $4. Recently, however, I saw some Valentine hankies in Houston that were marked $9 and $15; I was lucky to find the same designs in Massachusetts a few weeks later for only $2 each. Price depends on the demand in a given area so it pays to shop around.

## WEDDING HANKIES

These exquisite handkerchiefs are white linen or silk with multiple rows of intricate lace. Usually there is more lace than fabric. Many of these date back to the early part of this century. Used infrequently and passed down in families from one generation to the next, they are prized possessions. I have seen them framed, with acid-free papers, in a collage that included a wedding invitation and some pressed flowers from the bridal bouquet along with other wedding memorabilia. Sometimes a bride will save her wedding hankie to make into a Christening cap for her firstborn child. These treasured hankies sell from $25 to as high as $100. There is one, on page 83, that has been made into a pincushion. It could also be made into a very special ringbearer's pillow.

**These three little kitten don't have any mittens but they do have pretty handkerchief dresses. Just one scalloped-edge hankie is required for each.**

## CHILDREN'S HANKIES

If you are lucky enough to find them, these brightly colored hankies are absolutely charming. There are not as many of them around, as children were apt to lose them. They include printed designs featuring nursery rhyme characters and sayings from Mother Goose and Little Golden Books, alphabets, numbers, animals, and cartoon or storybook characters of the day. Many collectors prize the Disney characters—Cinderella, Mickey Mouse, Uncle Scrooge, and Pinnochio. Children's hankies can be expensive and chances are that you won't want to cut them up, but one or two can be adorable sewn on the bib of a child's overalls or as the center of a crib quilt. Prices start at $25 and go as high as $75 or more, depending on the rarity of the hankie.

## PATRIOTIC, SOUVENIR, AND NOVELTY HANKIES

Handkerchiefs have been printed for all kinds of special events. Early political handkerchiefs are highly valued (a "Win With Ike" might sell for $75) but there are more recent political handkerchiefs that will appreciate in value over time.

Serious collectors look for handkerchiefs that either have dates printed on them or can be dated by the event that they represent. World's Fair hankies are a good example. Bandanna print hankies from the 1930s with radio personalities, such as Tom Mix and the Lone Ranger, can be found.

Also from the 1930s through the 1950s are souvenir hankies with names of cities, states, and landmarks. If you travel (or have friends that do), you may want to collect these. You will see novelty handkerchiefs with calendars, maps, calorie charts, and horoscopes as well as special occasion message hankies that say "Thank You," "Bon Voyage," "Happy Birthday," or simply "Mother."

These special hankies can be displayed on a coffee table or desktop under a glass. I have some embroidered silk hankies displayed this way on a bedside table; the fun of it is that you can keep changing them around.

## TIPS TO REMEMBER

If you're planning a project that requires a number of hankies, all the same size, be sure to carry a sample hankie with you to match against. A handkerchief that has been laundered could be slightly smaller than one that was never out of the box. I once made the mistake of purchasing two dozen look-alike florals only to discover, when I got home, that only eight of them actually matched up. Handkerchiefs from different manufacturers or different "runs" of the same design may vary slightly. For example, Pat Gardner and I each have the same Tammis Keefe Christmas hankie (the one that Pat used in her

**Mix and match floral-print and crocheted-edge handkerchiefs, fill them with potpourri, and tie with pretty ribbons. Display a bouquet of them in a pretty basket. Make them by the dozen to use as party favors or to sell at church bazaars.**

wall hanging on page 85) except that mine measures 14¹/₂ inches (37cm) square and hers measures 12 inches (30.5cm). Prices of designer hankies range from $8 to $15.

Pay attention to the edges: It's not easy to join scalloped edges to straight edges. Does it matter to you if all the scallops are the same size? Look to see if there's a rolled hem that can easily be removed to provide a seam allowance.

Any handkerchief will cost more if it's still in the original box; it will probably be part of a set of three. Often, the boxes themselves are worth collecting. Some people want the actual cardboard boxes that the handkerchiefs came in; others are interested in the decorative fabric or wood containers that were purchased separately. Some handkerchief holders, are made of padded satin and other delicate

fabrics, and tie with ribbon to close. Less frequently seen are crocheted handkerchief holders, which are comprised of a square of solid crochet on the bottom and ribbon-threaded criss-crossed strips of crochet on top. You can slip several folded hankies neatly into the holder, under the crisscross strips.

Yard sales and estate sales are a good source for buying handkerchiefs. Looking through a basket or box of carefully preserved hankies can be a treasure trove and often presents a vivid picture of the woman who saved them.

Handkerchiefs are one of the best-kept secrets around. Just think, you can still buy any of the ones described here at very reasonable cost, whereas one new cotton handkerchief, with a designer name, is as much as $24 at department stores.

# Handkerchief Wreath

**Size:** Approximately 17 inches (43cm) in diameter

## What You'll Need

▶ 25 floral-print handkerchiefs
▶ Styrofoam® plastic foam wreath 12 inches (30.5cm) in
  diameter
▶ Heavy thread
▶ Iron and spray starch
▶ Straight pins
▶ 1 yard (1m) grosgrain ribbon 1 inch (2.5cm) wide, for covering
  sides of wreath form
▶ 4-inch (10cm) length of narrow ribbon, for hanging loop
▶ White craft glue
▶ Sharp pencil

## What To Do

1 Use a sharp pencil to poke a hole all the way through the
  wreath form. Rotate pencil gently after poking it in, to gradually
  expand the hole slightly. Repeat all around the wreath form, keeping holes 1 inch (2.5cm) apart.

2 To make the hanging loop, fold narrow ribbon crosswise in
  half. Pin ends to outer edges of wreath form. Glue grosgrain
  ribbon around outer edges of the wreath form which will also
  cover the loop ends.

3 Launder handkerchiefs and press with spray starch. Lay each
  hankie flat, then pick it up from the center, holding center
  together for a couple of inches and forming a flowery shape at
  edges. Pull the center ("stem" end) taut. Tightly wrap heavy thread
  around the handkerchief halfway between the center and the
  edges; tie thread ends to fasten off.

4 Push the center of each handkerchief through a hole in the
  wreath form, using eraser end of the pencil. Gently pull
  handkerchief through hole until tied threads lie against the
  back surface of the wreath form. You may need to twist the hankie
  gently as you pull the fabric through hole. Fill all the holes with
  handkerchiefs in this manner.

5 Turn the wreath to the wrong side and pin the centers of the
  handkerchiefs flat against the wreath form. On the right side,
  gently fluff each handkerchief for the fullest effect.

# Floral-Print Tablecloth/Quilt

**Size:** Approximately $48^{1}/_{2}$ x $78^{1}/_{2}$ inches (123 x 200cm),
not including handkerchief-points edging

## What You'll Need

▶ 15 same-size floral-print handkerchiefs, approximately 12 inches
  (31cm) square, for the quilt blocks
▶ 16 scalloped-edged handkerchiefs, approximately $16^{1}/_{2}$ inches
  (42cm) square, for the edging
▶ Preshrunk, tightly woven cotton fabrics 44 inches (112cm) wide:
  $4^{1}/_{2}$ yards (4.5m) solid green, for backing, corner blocks, and
  sashing squares; $2^{1}/_{2}$ yards (2.3m) each solid white, for quilt
  blocks, and green calico, for borders and sashing
▶ Quilt batting
▶ Sewing thread to match fabrics
▶ Quilting thread in assorted colors
▶ 8 large quilter's safety pins
▶ Large sheet of tracing paper
▶ Dressmaker's tracing (transfer) paper
▶ Dry, ballpoint pen
▶ Quilting hoop
▶ Sewing and quilting needles
▶ Iron and spray starch

## What To Do

1 Before beginning, launder all hankies, spray-starch lightly, and press.

2 Cut fabric pieces, referring to the assembly diagram; these dimensions include $^1/_4$-inch (6mm) seam allowances. For quilt blocks (A), cut fifteen $14^1/_2$-inch (37cm) squares from white fabric. For backing, cut and piece green fabric into a rectangle 50 x 80 inches (127 x 203cm). Use remaining green fabric to cut four 3-inch (8cm) squares, for corner blocks (F), and eight $1^1/_2$-inch (4cm) squares, for sashing squares (C). From green calico, cut 2 strips $2^3/_4$ x 80 inches (7 x 203cm), for long borders (D); 2 strips $2^3/_4$ x 50 inches (7 x 127cm), for short borders (E); and 22 strips $1^1/_2$ x $14^1/_2$ inches (4 x 37cm), for sashing strips (B).

3 To assemble the quilt top, lay out the pieces to correspond with the assembly diagram. Throughout the assembly, pin pieces together with right sides facing and adjacent, raw edges even, and sew, using $^1/_4$-inch (6mm) seam allowances. Working in horizontal rows, first piece together each of the 5 quilt block rows and vertical sashing strips: A, B, A, B, A. Next, piece together the horizontal sashing strips and sashing squares: B, C, B, C, B—4 rows total. Press seam allowances toward the darker-colored fabrics, then replace each pieced row in the layout. Taking care to match seams, stitch the horizontal rows together. Press seam allowances in the same manner as before.

4 To add the borders, first trim D and E strips to correspond to the exact measurements of the long and short sides of quilt top, respectively. Join a D strip to each long edge of quilt top, pinning and stitching in the same manner as before. Join an F square to each end of E, then attach along short sides of quilt, taking care to match seams at the corners.

5 To make the handkerchief-points edging, fold each of the 16 scalloped-edged handkerchiefs diagonally in half, with wrong side in. Pin foldlines to edges of quilt top, arranging 3 handkerchiefs along each short side and 5 along each long side. Space evenly, overlapping as necessary. Machine-baste $^1/_4$ inch (6mm) from edges all around. Pin the free corners of the handkerchiefs to the quilt top, toward the center, so they don't get caught in the stitching later.

6 To assemble the quilt, spread out the quilt batting smoothly on a large, flat surface. Center the backing, right side up, on batting. Center the quilt top, right side down, over that. Baste the layers together, then machine-stitch around, $^1/_4$ inch from quilt top edges, leaving an opening of approximately 12 inches (31cm) for turning. Trim the edges of backing and batting to match the quilt

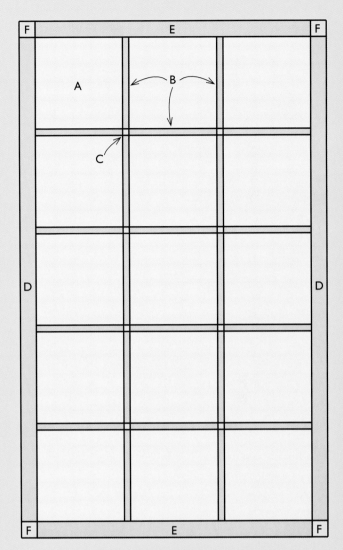

**ASSEMBLY DIAGRAM FOR TABLECLOTH/QUILT**

top, and clip into seam allowances across the corners. Turn quilt to right side. Turn open edges to inside and slipstitch closed.

7 To appliqué the handkerchiefs in place and machine-quilt at the same time, first smooth the quilt and fasten with safety pins at each sashing square, to keep the layers from shifting. Center a handkerchief on each quilt block. Pin handkerchiefs in place. Topstitch or zigzag-stitch around the edges of each handkerchief; work from the center outward all around, rolling and unrolling the quilt as necessary to gain access to all areas. Use thread to match quilt top fabrics and green bobbin thread. Next, remove the safety pins and straightstitch along the seams of each sashing strip, and along the inside edges of the border.

8 To hand-quilt a hearts design on the handkerchief blocks, first complete the actual-size quarter pattern as follows: Fold a 14-inch (36cm) square of tracing paper in half horizontally and then vertically, creasing sharply each time. Open the tracing paper, and lay one quarter of it over the pattern with the creases along

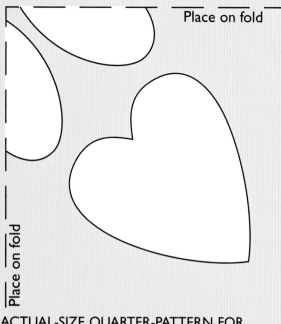

Place on fold

Place on fold

## ACTUAL-SIZE QUARTER-PATTERN FOR HAND-QUILTING TABLECLOTH/QUILT

the long dash lines. Trace the pattern. Rotate the tracing paper, and trace the pattern onto the other 3 quadrants of the creased tracing paper.

9 Pin the quilting pattern over each A block, and slip dressmaker's tracing paper, ink side down, in between. Go over the hearts design with a dry ballpoint pen to transfer. Remove pattern and dressmaker's tracing paper. Place each block in a hoop and use quilting thread in a color to complement each handkerchief. Referring to sewing how-to's in General Directions, Chapter Eight, quilt with small, even running stitches over pattern markings.

# Wedding Hankie Pincushion

**Size:** 4$\frac{1}{2}$ inches (11.5cm) square, not including 3$\frac{3}{4}$-inch (9.5cm) flange all around

## What You'll Need

▸ Lacy wedding handkerchief or other decorative hankie with lace border [the one shown is 12 inches (31cm) square]
▸ Small scrap of cotton or linen to match handkerchief, for backing
▸ Sewing thread to match handkerchief
▸ Small amount of polyester fiberfill, for stuffing
▸ Sewing needle and pins

## What To Do

1 Measure the center section of your handkerchief, to determine the size of the desired square cushion. Cut fabric $\frac{3}{8}$ inch (1cm) larger all around than these measurements.

2 Turn backing fabric edges $\frac{3}{8}$ inch (1cm) to the wrong side and press. Pin to the center of handkerchief, wrong sides facing. Slipstitch around 3 sides of the fabric and the corners of the fourth. Stuff plumply with fiberfill, then slipstitch to close.

# Holiday Handkerchief Angel

**Size:** Approximately 11 inches (28cm) tall

## What You'll Need

▸ 2 Christmas-print handkerchiefs, for head and dress (it helps to have a white center on one to use for the head area)
▸ Lacy white handkerchief for wings
▸ Styrofoam® plastic foam ball 1 inch (2.5cm) in diameter, for head
▸ Liquid starch
▸ Satin ribbon $\frac{1}{8}$ inch (3mm) wide: 1 yard (1m) red, $\frac{1}{4}$ yard (23cm) white
▸ Small amounts of dried gyp (or Baby's Breath) and Spanish moss, for hair and halo
▸ White glue
▸ Plastic wrap

## What To Do

1 Mix $^1/_2$ cup of liquid starch with 1 cup of water. Immerse hand-kerchiefs in this solution. Squeeze out well. Lay flat on a piece of plastic wrap to dry. When dry, sprinkle with water and use a press cloth to iron smooth.

2 Lay the smaller handkerchief right side down on tabletop. Place second handkerchief right side down, diagonally, on top of the first. Place Styrofoam ball on the center. Cut red ribbon in half and use both strands together. Gather handkerchiefs around ball and wrap tightly with ribbon. Tie a bow and move it to smoothest side of ball, for front.

3 To make the wings, fold accordion pleats down center of lace handkerchief, and pinch tightly. Tie with the center of white ribbon. Tie ribbon ends together for a hanging loop, if desired, or make a bow. Glue wings to back of angel, below head.

4 Place small amount of glue on top of head and press gyp in place, for hair. Make a ring of Spanish moss around your finger, and glue on top, for halo.

# Christmas Stockings

**Size:** 8 inches (20.5cm) long

## What You'll Need for Each

▶ 1 or more Christmas handkerchiefs, for stocking front and back
▶ Handkerchief with embroidered holiday motif, scalloped or crocheted edge, for cuff and trim
▶ White linen fabric, 10 x 20 inches (26 x 52cm), for lining
▶ Sewing thread to match fabric and handkerchiefs
▶ Fusible batting

## What To Do

1 Enlarge the pattern for the small stocking on page 62 of Quilts chapter. *Solid lines on this pattern represent stitching lines.* Before cutting out pattern, add $^1/_4$ inch (6mm) all around for seam allowance.

2 For stocking front, pin pattern to handkerchief, arranging on design to best advantage, and cut out. Reverse the pattern to cut a mirror image for the stocking back, from the same handker-chief or a second handkerchief, and cut out.

3 Then cut a front and a back piece from linen, for lining. Cut the $^1/_2$-inch (13mm) seam allowance from the pattern and use this revised pattern to cut 1 piece of fusible batting for either the front or back lining piece. Center batting on matching lining piece and iron to fuse.

4 To add a toe or heel section, refer to photograph for sugges-tions. Cut and position a section to fit over the area you wish to decorate. Trim excess fabric away from stocking front and turn any raw edges under; press and slipstitch in place.

5 To assemble stocking, pin handkerchief stocking front and back together with right sides facing and edges even. Sew around sides and foot with $^1/_4$-inch (6mm) seam allowances. Repeat for lining. Turn stocking right side out and insert lining with wrong sides facing and seams and toes matching up. Turn all top edges $^1/_2$ inch (13mm) to wrong side but leave unstitched.

6 To make a cuff, cut an area of embroidered, crocheted, or patterned handkerchief in a shape and depth that will accent-uate the design and is the same width as the stocking top front (and also back, if desired) plus $^1/_4$ inch (6mm) on each short side for seam allowance. Hem sides of cuff and bottom, if necessary.

7 Pin cuff to stocking with top edge inserted $^1/_2$ inch (13mm) between lining and stocking front. Slipstitch all around the inside top stocking edge to secure lining, handkerchief stocking, and cuff in place.

8 To make a hanging loop, cut a $1^1/_2$ x 5-inch (3cm x 12.5cm) strip from a finished edge of handkerchief remnant and fold lengthwise in half, wrong sides together. Fold crosswise in half and stitch ends to stocking front, at cuff level, lining up with the heel as shown in photo at left.

# Merry Christmas Wall Hanging

**Size:** As shown, 18$^1$/$_2$ inches (47cm) square

## What You'll Need

▶ 1 Christmas-print handkerchief for center medallion [one shown is 12-inches (30.5cm) square]

▶ $^1$/$_4$ yard (.25m) each 44-inch (112cm) wide cotton print fabrics, for borders to frame handkerchief: 2 Christmas prints for the pieced border blocks, a red/green stripe for outer border, and a green calico print for the 2 narrow borders

▶ 20-inch (51cm) square fabric of your choice, for backing

▶ Sewing thread to match fabrics

▶ Traditional quilt batting, 20 inches (51cm) square

▶ 19-inch (48.5cm) length of wide bias binding, for casing

▶ Sewing and quilting needles, pins

## What To Do

*Note: The following directions call for "framing" a 12-inch (30.5 cm) square handkerchief with borders, leaving an 11$^1$/$_4$-inch (29cm) square center showing. If the size of your handkerchief is much smaller or larger, adjust the number or width of the narrow borders, and/or the number of joined border blocks, striving for an odd number, so same fabric is in all corners.*

1 Dimensions of pieces to be cut all include $^1$/$_4$-inch (6mm) seam allowances. Unless otherwise indicated, pin all pieces with right sides facing and edges even, and sew, leaving $^1$/$_4$-inch (6mm) seam allowances. Press after each step, pressing seam allowances toward the darker fabric.

2 Expand or trim handkerchief to obtain an 11$^3$/$_4$-inch (30cm) square. If there is a rolled hem on your handkerchief, rip it out carefully to create extra seam allowance, wash the handkerchief, and press it. If necessary, trim off the rolled edge of the handkerchief.

3 Prepare the green calico fabric for the narrow borders by first cutting it, along the grain, into strips 1 inch (2.5cm) wide. Then, for inside border that frames the handkerchief, cut 2 strips each the same length as 1 handkerchief side. Pin 1 to each of 2 opposite sides of hankie. Stitch together. Unfold and press. Measure along remaining 2 sides, including the 2 borders, and cut 2 strips to fit this total measurement. Then join and press these strips in the same manner as the first 2 to form a frame on all sides of the handkerchief.

4 For pieced block border of Christmas prints, cut 32 2$^1$/$_4$-inch (6cm) squares, 16 from each print, centering motifs on each square. Alternate Christmas print blocks around the framed handkerchief, being sure to keep any figural designs vertical. Join the blocks for the top and bottom, then stitch to the framed handkerchief. Repeat with block borders at each side.

5 Referring to Step 3, add another narrow border of green calico.

6 To assemble wall hanging, place backing right side down, batting on top, and bordered handkerchief, right side up, centered on top of that. Baste layers in place.

7 To quilt, work from the center outward. To hand-quilt, make small, even running stitches to outline areas, as desired, or $^1$/$_8$ inch (3mm) from seams. Or, if you prefer, machine-quilt, stitching right on the seam.

　　Trim batting and backing to $^3$/$_4$ inch (2cm) beyond outer narrow border.

8 To make a casing for hanging, cut a length of wide bias binding to fit across top back of wall hanging. Hem ends of bias binding. Pin to back of wall hanging along top edge, centered between sides.

9 To finish wall hanging, cut striped fabric into four 2$^1$/$_2$ x 20-inch (6.5 x 51cm) binding strips, so that stripes run crosswise. Pin a binding strip along long raw edge of each calico border, with right sides facing and an equal amount of striped fabric extending at either end. Stitch through all layers, leaving $^1$/$_4$-inch (6mm) seam allowance and beginning and ending $^1$/$_4$ inch (6mm) from ends of border; do not continue stitching into the seam allowance areas. To miter the binding at each corner, pin the ends of adjacent border strips together, right sides facing, and hand-stitch from where the machine sewing starts/ends outward at a 45 degree angle. Press. Also press the long raw edges of the binding $^1$/$_4$ inch (6mm) to the wrong side.

Bring the binding over the batting and backing edges to the back of the wall hanging, and pin in place. Fold the corners neatly in back. Slipstitch the pressed edges in place, catching the top of the casing as well. Slipstitch the bottom edge of the casing, leaving the ends open so a rod or dowel may be slipped through, for hanging.

# Have-A-Heart Pillows

## Size: As shown, 14, 16, and 18 inches (37.5, 41, and 47.5cm) square

## What You'll Need
▶ Valentine handkerchiefs, print and/or embroidered
▶ Ready-made pillows, *or* the following items for making your own:
▶ $^5/_8$ yard (.6m) red or white cotton sateen fabric
▶ $2^1/_4$ yards (2.1m) red, ready-made piping
▶ Red, white sewing thread
▶ Square, knife-edge pillow forms to fit, or polyester fiberfill for stuffing
▶ Optional: Red picot-edge ribbon, $^3/_8$-inch (1cm) wide, for trim
▶ Sewing needle and pins
▶ Sewing machine with zipper foot attachment

## What To Do
1 Purchase, or make, your pillow top at least $1^1/_2$ inch (4cm) larger all around than the largest handkerchief that you plan to use. Choose a background color for the pillow top that contrasts with the color of the edging.

2 To make your own pillow, measure the largest handkerchief that you plan to use, then cut 1 square of cotton for the pillow top and a matching one for the pillow back at least $1^1/_2$ inch (4cm) larger on all sides than the measurement of the handkerchief.

3 How you mount your handkerchiefs on the pillow top will depend on your choice of hankies: Some will look fine as is; in other cases, you might want to fold them to make the most of an attractive border. Position handkerchiefs, right side up, on right side of pillow top until you're satisfied with the arrangement, then, beginning with the largest handkerchief, pin in place and slipstitch to pillow top around all edges. Repeat with remaining handkerchiefs.

*Pillow in the foreground:* Select 1 large, print handkerchief with interesting graphics and stitch in place. As the border of this hankie is red, it shows up best on a white pillow top. Add red piping to pick up the color scheme.

*Pillow on bench, far left:* You will need 3 embroidered handkerchiefs to form a collage on this pillow top. First, stitch one, with a design concentrated on the side, to the pillow top. Cut a second, with a corner motif, into a square and stitch in place lower left. Cut a third, on the diagonal, and stitch in place at top left with the lace-edged point overlapping the bottom square. Cover all outside edges with picot-edge ribbon.

*Pillow on bench, second from left:* Stitch 1 hankie with a white lacy border to a red pillow top. Center an embroidered hankie on top, with all scalloped corners folded to the middle. Stitch in place and add a small red bow where the corners meet.

*Pillow on bench, second from right:* To create this dimensional effect, layer the hankies as follows: Begin with a large print handkerchief; center a smaller embroidered hankie on top of it. Stitch both in place. Finally, fold an embroidered hankie with a decorative edge as if you were folding it to put in a pocket; tuck the bottom, folded end under, and stitch in place, as shown in photo.

*Pillow on bench, far right:* Stitch 1 large print handkerchief to the pillow top. Place a smaller, contrasting one on the diagonal over it and stitch in place.

4 If you are making your own pillow, add piping after handkerchiefs are stitched in place on pillow top. To do so, pin piping around pillow top, right sides facing and edges even (cording will be toward the center front). Overlap piping ends by 1 inch (2.5cm). Cut open one end of piping and remove 1 inch (2.5cm) of cotton cording from inside. Fold under $^1/_4$ inch (6mm) of piping fabric at this end, then position this section over opposite end of piping; pin to secure. Baste piping in place; using a zipper foot, machine-stitch close to the cording all around.

**5** To assemble pillow, place pillow top on pillow back, with right sides facing and edges even. Using a zipper foot, stitch around 3 sides and corners of the fourth, slightly to the inside of previous stitching line for piping. Clip into seam allowances at corners. Turn pillow cover to right side, and insert pillow form or stuffing. Turn open edges to inside and slipstitch closed.

# Three Little Kittens

**Size:** 14 inches (36cm) tall

## What You'll Need for Each

▶ Large, scalloped-edge, floral-print handkerchief [one shown is 16 inches (41cm) square]
▶ $^1/_2$ yard (.5m) small print cotton fabric in colors to match handkerchief
▶ Sewing thread to match fabric and handkerchief
▶ 1 yard (1m) ribbon $^1/_4$ to $^3/_8$ inch (6mm to 1cm) wide, for drawstring neckline
▶ 6-strand embroidery floss, for facial features
▶ Polyester fiberfill, for stuffing
▶ Large sheet of tracing paper
▶ Sewing and embroidery needles
▶ Small safety pin

## What To Do

**1** Enlarge kitten pattern on page 97, onto tracing paper, and cut out. Pattern includes $^1/_4$-inch (6mm) seam allowances.

**2** Use this pattern to cut a front and back kitten shape from the print fabric.

**3** Embroider a face on the front, referring to pattern markings and using 4 strands of floss in embroidery needle. For eyes, make a French knot. For the nose and mouth, use outline stitches.

**4** To assemble doll, pin front and back together with right sides facing, matching edges to be joined. Sew $^1/_4$ inch (6mm) from edges, leaving open between **O** marks as indicated on pattern—but only on 1 side of the kitten. Clip into the seam allowances along curves and at angles, as indicated on pattern. Turn right side out through opening. Use the eraser end of a pencil to push ears, arms, and legs out, and to push stuffing in. When doll is plumply stuffed, turn open edges $^1/_4$ inch to inside and slipstitch closed.

**5** To make the dress, cut handkerchief in half. On each half, turn cut edges $^1/_2$ inch (13mm) to wrong side, and press. Stitch close to raw edge, forming a casing. On one half, for dress front, cut 2 small slits in the right side of the casing at the center and $^1/_2$ inch (13mm) apart. Place dress front on remaining handkerchief half, which will be dress back, with wrong sides facing and casing edges even. Fasten a small safety pin to one end of ribbon and guide the ribbon into one casing slit, all the way around through the dress back casing, then around to the dress front casing and out the second slit.

**6** Slip the dress over the kitten doll and pull the ribbon ends to gather the neckline casing. Tie the ribbon ends in a bow. Pin the dress front and back together below the kitten's arms and slipstitch to join sides of dress.

# Sachets

**Size:** Approximately 8 inches (20.5cm) long

## What You'll Need for Each

▶ Scalloped-edge floral handkerchief
▶ Crocheted-edge handkerchief
▶ Approximately 4 tablespoons potpourri
▶ 6-inch (15cm) square of cheesecloth for each sachet
▶ $^5/_8$ yard (.6m) each: ribbons in assorted widths to match handkerchief colors
▶ Spray starch

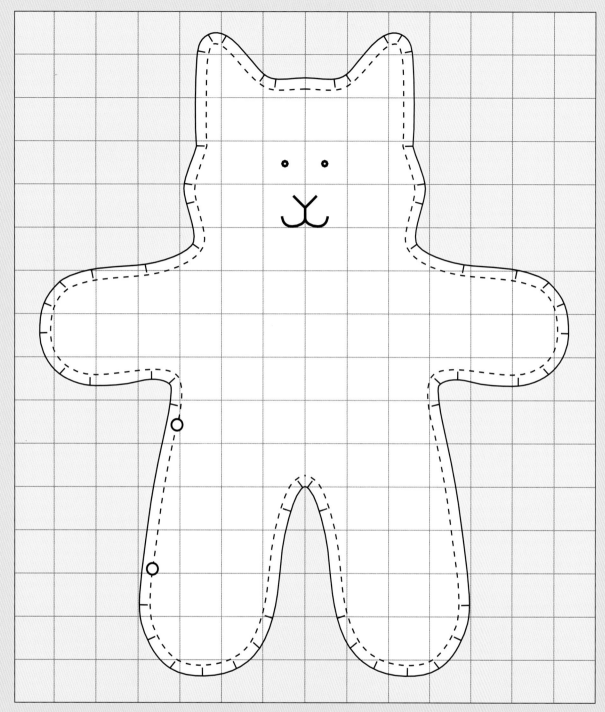

REDUCED PATTERN FOR KITTEN DOLL        Each Square Equals 1 Inch (2.5cm).

## What To Do

1 Launder, spray-starch, and press handkerchiefs. Place the smaller one wrong side up, on a tabletop. Center the larger one, wrong side up, on top of the first.

2 Spoon potpourri into the middle of a square of cheesecloth. Gather the edges together and tie tightly with thread to secure. Place this ball in the center of the 2 layered hankies. Bring the edges of both handkerchiefs up, gather them together, and wrap and tie with thread or a narrow rubber band.

3 Tie 1 or more pieces of ribbon tightly around the gathered handkerchiefs, close to the top of the potpourri ball. Fluff out the edges as shown in photo.

Brighten up a dining area with fruit and floral patterns. A tablecloth and matching napkins are the main ingredients for this window treatment—the napkins are the valance. Place mats are folded kitchen towels lined with batting.

# Chapter Six

# Kitchen Linens

Printed tablecloths and towels characterized by vibrant colors and bold designs were once as commonplace in American households as paper napkins are today. Manufactured in vast numbers, these linens appeared on the scene in the 1920s but really hit their heyday in the 1930s and 1940s. Their vivid, colorfast designs make them attractive for many decorating projects.

It's the berries! This strawberry
print tablecloth was in excellent
condition and just the right size for
a small coverlet. Pillow sham is a
towel. Blue-and-white gingham
ruffled edging ties it all together.

*I*n the days before microwave ovens and America's love affair with fast foods, an evening meal could take hours to prepare. On weekdays, families often enjoyed their home-cooked dinners in the kitchen and on the kitchen table would be a cheerful tablecloth. These everyday cloths are now valued for their retro charm and nostalgic appeal.

## A LITTLE HISTORY

Made of linen, cotton, and rayon-cotton blends, these fabrics were produced in the United States as well as imported from England, Holland, and Japan and sold in dime-stores, dry-goods stores, and department stores all across the United States. Families bought several and changed them frequently and seasonally.

Original prices averaged between $1 and $2 for a tablecloth. Even high-end manufacturers that could afford to advertise in a 1942 issue of *House & Garden* offered mail-order tablecloths for only $1.69 and $2.69, including postage. Matching napkins could be purchased for 25 cents each. A Christmas set at $2.98 was listed as "a perfect hostess gift—appropriate for bridge parties, luncheons, tea—any occasion from break-fast to a midnight snack. An ideal war-time gift."

**Napkins were used to make up the reversible cat ornaments on this grapevine wreath but towels or tablecloth scraps would work as well.**

I recently saw several tablecloths with their original paper labels at Laura Fisher/Antique Quilts and Americana in NYC. One label read "Hand Printed, Cotton & Spun Rayon, Fast Colors, Luncheon Cloth" and although it was a souvenir cloth with a map of Mexico it was made in Japan.

A few tablecloths have designers' signatures; Laura has one showing forty-eight states with the words "Pageant of the States" and the name Tom Lamb. A couple of other designer names you'll see include Virginia Zito and Vera. Some linens will have copyright marks with and without dates. I see more copyrights from the 1940s, but that may just be coincidence.

Cathy Cook, a collector in New York City, tells me that "Linens from the 1920s most frequently had deco or arts-and-crafts inspired geometric motifs." By the 1930s, there were florals and pastel colors, including soft peach, lavenders, and pale blues. Adds Cook, "Fruit and flowers became bolder and larger in scale in the mid-1940s coupled with bright borders. Later in the decade, souvenir maps, south-of-the-border designs, and cowboys became popular. Abstract patterns (especially stripes) were popular in the 1950s along with images of kitchen implements. Avocado and earth tones were prevalent."

Designs were influenced by casual dinnerware patterns, often available in more than one color. Fiestaware® and Lu-Ray® are good examples. Therefore, you can see the same tablecloth pattern in more than one color combination.

These vintage cloths were mass-produced and were made to stand up to wear. Because of that, quite a few of them are available at flea markets. Square and rectangular, they come in a variety of sizes, which makes them ideal for converting into pillows, curtains, toys, and even slipcovers.

## SHOPPING FOR TABLECLOTHS

Fruit and floral patterned cloths, towels, and nap-kins are the most plentiful. Fruit motifs include apples, peaches, pears, plums, cherries, grapes, pineapples, bananas, and all kinds of berries. Colors are primary reds, yellows, oranges, blues, and greens on white or ecru backgrounds. Some Southwest fiesta-style designs include red and

green peppers and an abundance of cactus coupled with festive terra-cotta pots and women in Carmen Miranda–influenced ruffled dresses.

Flowers come in all shapes, sizes, and species. You may find small sprigs of red or yellow flowers scattered against a white background with just a simple border stripe or you might find full-blown poppies, dahlias, sunflowers, roses, or tulips against a latticework background as in the one that was used for the ruffled pillow below. A mix of brilliant colors is most commonplace. However, there are some stylish two-tone patterns: I have one that has a magenta center with drop-out white dogwood flowers and then an outside stripe of the same magenta. It's not unusual to see variations of this style particularly in shades of blues, pinks, and reds.

Fruit and floral tablecloths, in good condition, range in price from $20 to $45. Brighter colors are more popular and more expensive than pastels. Cloths with small tears, minor holes, or some stains can be found for $7 to $15.

Naturally, never-used tablecloths in pristine condition with the original label intact are more valuable and can cost anywhere from $45 to $95 or maybe even more.

### TOWELS AND NAPKINS

Kitchen towels are less available, maybe because they wore out faster, and

prices range from $8 to $20. The designs will repeat the same motifs as the tablecloths but are positioned differently. A tablecloth will usually have a center or overall design combined with a border which can be even more elaborate than the center. Towels generally feature a design centered on the front (the part of the towel that shows when it is folded) with a simpler pattern around the edges. For example, there may be a floral at the front and then a border comprised of a couple of the floral leaves. This does not imply that the rest of the fabric is left undecorated; it's not. There will be a sprinkling of smaller flowers, fruit, or other motifs scattered on the background. An average size for a towel is 15 x 27 inches (38 x 68.9cm) or 13 x 28 inches (33 x 71cm); some are larger. Due to years of laundering, there are many variations. Some towels fit the rods of interior window shutters and are appealing in a kitchen or family room.

If you're lucky, you may find a tablecloth with a matching set of napkins. If you do, the price will reflect the uniqueness and will probably start at $35 or $45, depending on the number of napkins. Napkins alone will be anywhere from $2 to $5 each or a set of 4 for $15. Napkin sizes range from 16 to 10 inches (41 to 25.5cm) and can be squares or rectangles. Napkins will have corner motifs, solid white or off-white centers, and often a simple border.

A single napkin can be perfect for a pillow top or several can be joined together for a patchwork quilt.

### SOUVENIR MAPS

You will see tablecloths printed for nearly every state. Americana dealer Laura Fisher says, "Buying a souvenir tablecloth on vacation then was like buying a T-shirt today." The most available states are the locales of the most popular vacation spots including Florida and California. If you look carefully at one of these cloths, you'll find that great care went into the design. A tablecloth from Florida might have symbols for landmark sights, such as a propeller plane at a military base to depict Pensacola; cigars for Tampa; circus characters for Sarasota, race cars for Daytona, and shrimp boats and water sports around the

**Two over-sized pillows are each made from an individual tablecloth. The center section is used for the pillow top and the border makes up the ruffle.**

Our lovely model, Annabelle, is wearing a sundress made from a table-cloth of summer fruit motifs. Eyelet caps the sleeves and the ribbon-print border is used for the bodice. Good news for moms is that it's not only easy to make but a cinch to toss into the washing machine.

A $4 holly-print tablecloth makes up into a cheerful tote bag, just right for holiday shopping. Our pleasantly plump teddy bear is stitched from a checkered tablecloth, which is also used to line the tote.

coast-line in addition to the traditional stereotypic palm trees and fish. A New York tablecloth might include line-art drawings of the Brooklyn Bridge, the Flatiron Building, the Statue of Liberty, the Frick, the Metropolitan Museum of Art, and even hospitals. There were a number of versions for many states. Some collectors concentrate on just one state to see how many different variations they can find. Most of these tourist cloths are bought to use as intended or to frame as art. They don't lend themselves as well to crafts projects because you'd be cutting through a map. However, find a pair from your home state and use them for curtains—or maybe even several sets from several states.

Prices on souvenir tablecloths range from $30 to $65 for the more common states and $75 to $150 for harder-to-find states or designs.

### HOLIDAY TABLECLOTHS

Special cloths were made for Christmas, and popular motifs include poinsettias, bells, holly, and pinecones. There are cloths with words such as "Seasons Greetings," "Joy" and "Noel" incorporated into the design, especially in borders. Fewer of these Christmas cloths are available—probably because they were used only a few weeks a year and at a season when fine linens were usually brought out to entertain company. Holiday cloths are not as sought after by collectors because of their limited uses (unless you specialize in collecting Christmas)

and often are reasonably priced. I bought 4 or 5 Christmas cloths, all priced under $15. A $4 purchase was torn in the center but there was enough fabric to use in a Christmas stocking and a tote bag. I am not aware of other holiday-specific designs although cloths with horns of plenty and fall foliage certainly suggest Thanksgiving, and some very patriotic red/white/blue scenes complete with steepled churches and flags might have been brought out for July 4th, Memorial Day, or Flag Day.

### TIPS TO REMEMBER

Serious collectors look for more than fruit and flowers. You might not want to purchase unusual (and often costlier) cloths to recycle but it's interesting to be able to recognize them when you see them. For example, there is a range of ethnic cloths, including African-American, Latin-American, and Native American.

A little more commonplace are regional cloths. Potted tulips with latticework hearts and stylized birds originate from Pennsylvania Dutch fraktur and stencil shapes. Western cloths feature cowboys, guns, horses, branding irons, and perhaps even a wood-grain pattern.

Another category of kitchen cloths are checks. Usually at least 1-inch (2.5cm) square, these checks come in blue, red, green, or aqua and white.

Depending on what you plan to make from your tablecloths, imperfections may not be a problem as there will still be a considerable amount of fabric to use. Napkins, towels, and smaller items such as place mats or runners do not have as much room to cut around so you'll want to be more discerning.

There's no reason not to simply enjoy tablecloths as tablecloths. Layer several, starting with the larger ones on the bottom, to make the most of colorful border designs.

To really play up the mood, set your table with vintage linens and dinnerware and serve foods of the times such as tuna casserole, grilled cheese sandwiches with root beer floats or TV dinners. Let the fun begin!

**Christmas cloths were used to stitch up these stockings. The striped cuff, at right, is actually the border of the tablecloth that was used to make the stocking at left.**

# Fruit-and-Floral Kitchen Set

**Size:** To fit

## What You'll Need

**For Curtains:**

▶ Printed tablecloth large enough to fit window:
  as shown, 54 inches (137.5cm) square

▶ 1¹/₂ yards (1.4m) old or new ball fringe

▶ Sewing thread to match cloth and trim

**For Valance:**

▶ 4 napkins: these are 16-inches (41cm) square

▶ Sewing thread to match

**For Both:**

▶ Double curtain rod

## What To Do

1 To make 2 curtain panels, cut tablecloth in half, using design to best advantage. Hem cut edges by folding ¹/₂ inch (13mm) to wrong side twice and machine-stitching.

2 For each panel, cut ball fringe 1 inch (2.5cm) longer than bottom edge. Fold ball fringe ends ¹/₂ inch (13mm) to wrong side, pin to bottom edge, and sew in place with tape portion on right side of curtain.

3 Make a casing at the top by hanging panel over curtain rod: With ball fringe at sill level, or where desired, fold top edge over curtain rod; pin in place. Trim excess fabric at top edge if necessary to ¹/₂ inch (13mm) beyond pins. Fold edge ¹/₂ inch (13mm) to wrong side and stitch across.

4 Slip curtain panels onto inside curtain rod (with hemmed edges on the outside if there is a border treatment, such as the red and blue stripes shown here).

5 To make valance, drape napkins diagonally over outside curtain rod, overlapping them and spacing them across so corners at the bottom form an even zigzag. Pin together 1 inch (2.5cm) below curtain rod. Slip off rod, and stitch along pins to create casing.

# Fold-and-Sew Place Mats

**Size:** Approximately 17 x 13 inches (43 x 33cm)

## What You'll Need for Each

▶ Printed kitchen towel, approximately
  17 x 27 inches (43 x 68.5cm)

▶ Fusible batting, approximately 17 x 13 inches (43 x 33cm)

▶ Sewing thread to match towel

## What To Do

1 Fold towels, crosswise, so that short ends meet at front center. Iron creases along fold lines.

2 Open towel and cut batting to fit within creases. Fuse batting in place. Fold towel ends over and machine-stitch ends and sides of place mat closed.

# Tie-Back Chair-Seat Pads

**Size:** To fit: as shown, 16 x 15 inches (41 x 38cm), not including ball fringe

## What You'll Need for Each

▶ Printed kitchen towel (or 1 tablecloth for all)
▶ Cotton fabric approximately 18 inches (46cm) square or another towel for bottom of cushion
▶ High-loft polyester batting, approximately 18 inches (46cm) square
▶ Approximately 1¹/₂ yards (1.4m) old or new ball fringe
▶ Sewing thread to match fabric and ball fringe
▶ Tracing paper, pencil, yardstick
▶ Sewing needle, straight pins

## What To Do

1 To make a pattern, spread a sheet of tracing paper over chair seat and trace around seat. Remove paper and use yardstick to even lines for straight edges; cut out. Pin pattern to towel. Adding ¹/₂ inch (13mm) all around for seam allowances, cut out seat-pad top. Cut out an identical piece for bottom of seat pad from fabric or another towel. Use the same pattern but do not add seam allowances to cut batting. Using remainder of towel and incorporating a finished long edge whenever possible, cut four 1¹/₂ x 17-inch (4 x 43cm) strips, for ties.

2 Pin batting to wrong side of seat-pad bottom, centering; baste to secure. Pin seat-pad top and bottom together, right sides facing and edges even. With ¹/₂-inch (13mm) seam allowances, stitch around all but back edge. Clip across seam allowances at front corners and turn pad to right side. Turn back edges ¹/₂ inch (13mm) to inside and pin.

3 To make ties, turn one long edge and one short edge of each strip ¹/₄ inch (6mm) to wrong side and press. Fold strip lengthwise into thirds, wrong side in, with folded edge on top. Stitch along folded top edge. Insert raw ends of 2 ties at each back corner of chair-seat pad. Stitch back edge closed.

4 For trim, pin ball fringe over seams around sides and front of chair-seat pad, turning ends of trim at back corners ¹/₄ inch (6mm) to wrong side. Slipstitch in place.

# Strawberry Coverlet and Pillow Sham

**Sizes: Coverlet,** 47 x 59 inches (119.5 x150cm), not including 4¹/₂-inch (11.5cm) wide ruffle all around; **Pillow Sham,** 16 x 26¹/₂ inches (41 x 67.5cm), not including 4¹/₂-inch (11.5cm) wide ruffle all around

## What You'll Need

**For Coverlet:**
▶ Printed tablecloth, 48 x 60 inches (122 x 152.5cm)
▶ 3 yards (3m) 44-inch (112cm) wide gingham fabric for ruffle
▶ 1³/₄ yards (1.6m) 54-inch (137cm) wide fabric, or 3¹/₂ yards (3.4m) standard-width fabric for backing
▶ High-loft batting, such as Fairfield Processing Corp.'s Poly-fil® Hi-Loft® Batting, 72 x 90 inches (183 x 229cm)

**For Pillow Sham:**
▶ Printed kitchen towel or runner to coordinate with tablecloth, at least 17 x 27¹/₂ inches (43 x 70cm)
▶ 2 yards (2m) 44-inch (112cm) wide gingham fabric for ruffle and backing
▶ Standard bed pillow

**For Both:**
▶ Sewing thread to match and contrast with fabrics

## What To Do

### COVERLET

**1** For ruffle, cut 10-inch (25.5cm) wide strips along the lengthwise grain of the gingham fabric. With right sides facing, join strips end to end to make a strip approximately 12 yards (12m) in length. Following trimming how-to's in the General Directions, Chapter Eight, make a folded ruffle and attach to the right side of the tablecloth, leaving $^1/_2$-inch (13mm) seam allowances.

**2** For backing, cut and piece gingham fabric as necessary to obtain a rectangle 2 inches (5cm) larger all around than tablecloth. Cut batting to same size.

**3** To assemble coverlet, spread backing wrong side up on a flat surface, with batting on top. Pin and baste together. Turn layers so backing is right side up and place tablecloth, wrong side up, on top. Stitch around along previous stitching line of ruffle, or $^1/_2$ inch (13mm) from raw edges; leave about 12 inches (31cm) open for turning. Trim seams to $^1/_4$ inch (6mm) and clip across seam allowances at corners. Turn coverlet to right side, and slipstitch opening closed.

**4** To prepare to quilt, work from the center and baste outward in all directions. Then, also working from the center out, machine- or hand-quilt along pattern design lines in the tablecloth, or as desired. Remove basting stitches.

### PILLOW SHAM

**1** For pillow top, trim kitchen towel so it measures 17 x 27$^1/_2$ inches (43 x 70cm). For backing, cut two 17 x 16$^1/_2$-inch (43 x 42cm) rectangles from gingham fabric.

**2** For ruffle, divide remainder of gingham fabric into 10-inch (25.5cm) wide strips cut along the grain. With right sides facing, join strips end to end, to make a strip approximately 4$^3/_4$ yards (4.7m) in length. Following trimming how-to's in the General Directions, Chapter Eight, make a folded ruffle and attach it to the right side of the towel, leaving $^1/_2$-inch (13mm) seam allowances.

**3** On each backing rectangle, turn one 17-inch (43cm) edge $^3/_4$ inch (2cm) to the wrong side twice, and machine-stitch to secure. Following pillow-making how-to's in the General Directions, Chapter Eight, make a knife-edge pillow with an overlapped back.

## Grapevine Wreath

**Size: Cats,** 5 inches (13cm) high by 5$^1/_2$ inches (14cm); **Wreath,** 16 inches (41cm) in diameter

## What You'll Need

▶ Printed kitchen napkins, towels, or tablecloth remnants
▶ Sewing thread to match
▶ Polyester fiberfill for stuffing
▶ Grapevine wreath, 16 inches (41cm) in diameter
▶ Glue gun and glue sticks
▶ Tracing paper, pencil, straight pins

## What To Do

**1** To make cats, trace the actual-size pattern on page 109 onto tracing paper. Pin pattern to towel and cut out 8 pieces with the tails going in the same direction. Pattern includes $^1/_4$-inch (6mm) seam allowances. Then reverse pattern and cut out 8 more cats in mirror image.

**2** Pin pieces together in pairs, with right sides facing. Sew all around, leaving $^1/_4$-inch (6mm) seam allowances and leaving areas unstitched between **O** marks as shown on pattern. Clip into seam allowances as indicated on pattern. To eliminate bulk, trim seam allowances close to stitches around ears and tail. Turn to right side.

**3** Stuff each cat with fiberfill. Use the eraser end of a pencil to push fiberfill into the ears, tail, and front paws. Turn in open edges and slipstitch closed.

**4** Arrange cats on wreath with tails pointing outward on either side. Apply hot glue to back of each cat, and press in place. (Or stitch in place if you prefer.)

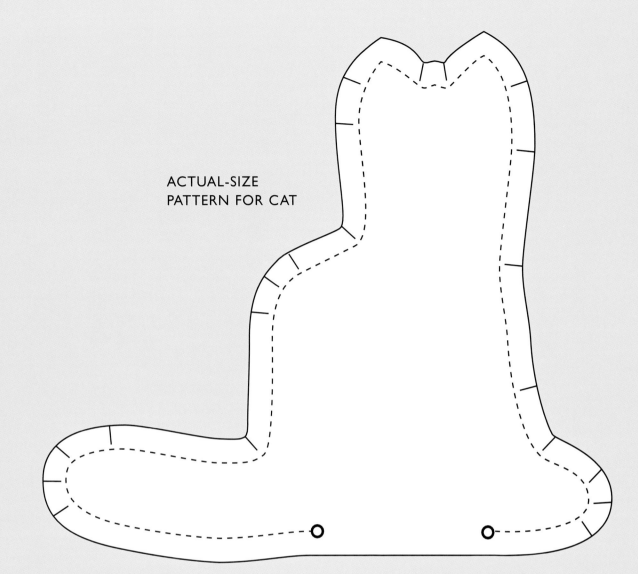

ACTUAL-SIZE
PATTERN FOR CAT

# Ruffled Pillows

**Sizes:** 18 and 20 inches (46 and 51cm) square, not including 4-inch (10cm) wide ruffle all around

## What You'll Need for Each

▶ Printed kitchen tablecloth
▶ Cotton fabric to coordinate with tablecloth, approximately 21 inches (54cm) square for pillow back (or, use remaining tablecloth, if large enough)
▶ Sewing thread to match
▶ Knife-edge pillow form, 18 or 20 inches (46 and 51cm) square

## What To Do

1 *For large pillow,* mark and cut a 21-inch (53.5cm) square from tablecloth for pillow top. Cut a same-size square from coordinating fabric or tablecloth, for pillow back. For ruffle, use remainder of tablecloth to cut 5-inch (13cm) wide strips, piecing as necessary to obtain a length of 165 inches (419cm). Following pillow-making and trimming how-to's in the General Directions, Chapter Eight, make a hemmed ruffle and baste to a knife-edge pillow top.

2 *For small pillow,* mark and cut a 19-inch (48.5cm) square from tablecloth for pillow top. Cut a same-size square from coordinating fabric or tablecloth, for pillow back. For ruffle, use remainder of tablecloth to cut 5-inch (13cm) wide strips, piecing as necessary to obtain a length of 144 inches (366cm). Make a hemmed ruffle, as indicated in the trimming how-to's in the General Directions, Chapter Eight.

3 To pleat the edge, (as on small pillow) rather than gathering it, begin at a crosswise seam. Measure $1^3/_4$ inches (4.5cm), then fold strip to wrong side; pin. Measure $^3/_4$ inch (2cm) from fold, and fold to right side. The two facing folds create an inverted

pleat. Continue in this manner, making $^3/_4$-inch (2cm) pleats every $1^3/_4$ inches (4.5cm) across entire length of ring. Machine-stitch close to the raw edge, securing the pleats. Pin ruffle to the pillow top, distributing pleats evenly all around but allowing for extra fabric in the corners. Referring to the pillow-making how-to's in the General Directions, Chapter Eight, make a knife-edge pillow with a closed back.

# Annabelle's Sundress

**Size:** Child's size 6–8; 31 inches (79cm) long from shoulder to hem

## What You'll Need
▶ Large printed tablecloth, at least 70 inches (178cm) in one direction
▶ $1^1/_2$ yards (1.4m) $4^1/_2$-inch (11.5cm) wide eyelet trim, for sleeves
▶ 1 package $^1/_2$-inch (13mm) wide, double-fold seam binding, for finishing neckline and armholes
▶ Sewing thread to match tablecloth and trim
▶ 8 buttons $^3/_8$-inch (1cm) in diameter

## What To Do
1 Cut dress pieces from tablecloth. Begin with the skirt, and cut the following rectangles: For skirt front, cut one 32 x $24^1/_2$ inches (81.5 x 62.5cm), with finished edge of tablecloth along one 32-inch (81.5cm) side. For skirt backs—left and right, cut two 19 x $24^1/_2$ inches (48.5 x 62.5cm), with finished edge of tablecloth along one 19-inch (48.5cm) edge. You will be using the finished edges for the hem of the skirt. Set these rectangles aside.

2 Enlarge patterns for front and back bodice pieces on page 111 and pin on remaining tablecloth fabric. Cut 2 bodice backs.

Fold remaining tablecloth fabric in half and place bodice-front pattern on fabric with long dash lines on fold. Cut out 1 bodice front.

3 Sew gathering stitches along top edges—opposite the finished hem edge—of front skirt piece. Gather each skirt back, but leave unstitched from center back edge for a distance of $4^1/_4$ inches (11cm); this area will be folded under and will contain the buttonholes, so it should remain flat and without gathers.

4 With right sides facing, pin bodice pieces to corresponding skirt pieces, pulling the skirt gathers to fit. Stitch the pieces together, $^3/_8$ inch (1cm) from empire waist edge. On the joined back pieces, turn the center back edges $1^1/_2$ inches (4cm) to wrong side twice; press.

5 With right sides facing, pin, then sew front and back pieces together at shoulders and along side seams. Press seams open and turn dress to right side. Now cut a $1^1/_4$-inch (3cm) quarter-circle or wedge into each top corner of skirt, which will extend the armhole openings below the bodice.

6 To finish neckline edge, pin one long, unfolded edge of bias tape to neckline, with right sides of tape and fabric facing, raw edges even, and $^3/_8$ inch (1cm) of bias tape extending at each end. Stitch along crease of bias tape. Clip into seam allowances along curves. Fold tape up and over to inside of dress, tucking tape ends in; slipstitch in place.

7 To make ruffled cap sleeves, cut eyelet trim in half. Sew gathering stitches along each piece, tapering the ends as shown in the diagram on page 111: Pull threads to gather. Pin trim to armhole, starting and ending at bottom of armhole, with right sides facing and gathering stitches $^1/_4$ inch (6mm) from armhole edges. Baste to secure; trim away excess eyelet fabric at the ends, beyond armhole. Starting at bottom of armhole, pin seam binding on top of eyelet, in the same way that neckline was bound, but stitch all the way around armhole, $^3/_8$ inch (1cm) from raw edges, rather than along the seam-binding crease. Clip into seam allowances along curves of armhole. Bring opposite edge of seam binding to inside of dress; stitch in place to secure.

8 Mark positions for buttonholes along the left side, $^3/_4$ inch (1cm) from folded center back edge: at the top of the bodice back, at the top of the skirt back, midway between them, and at 3-inch (8cm) increments all along skirt back. Make buttonholes, referring to instructions for your sewing machine. Test-fit dress on child. Determine overlap of back opening for best fit. Sew on buttons to correspond with buttonholes. Hem skirt if desired.

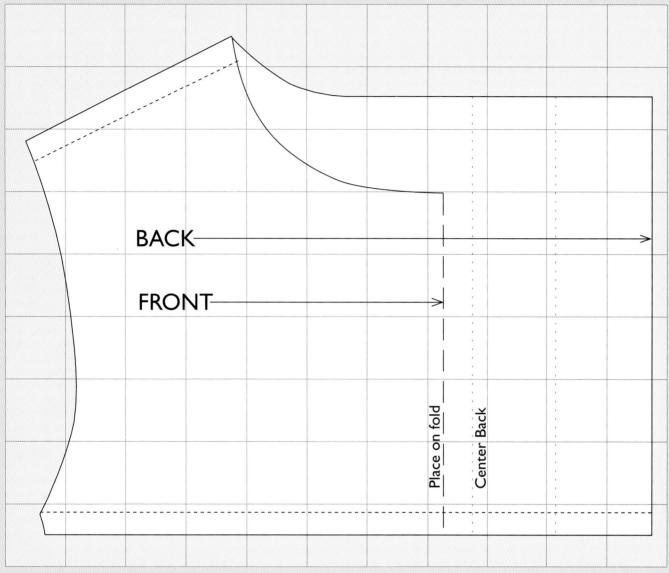

BACK

FRONT

Place on fold

Center Back

REDUCED PATTERNS FOR BODICE PIECES

Each square equals 1 inch (2.5cm)

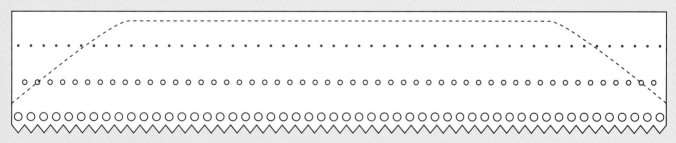

DIAGRAM FOR GATHERING EYELET ON SUNDRESS SLEEVES

# Christmas Cloth Tote

**Size:** 16¹/₂ x 13 x 3¹/₄ inches (42 x 33 x 8.5cm)

## What You'll Need

▶ Christmas-print tablecloth, at least 44 inches (112cm) square
▶ Red-and-white cotton jacquard tablecloth for lining
▶ Sewing thread to match fabrics
▶ 2 yards (2m) fusible batting
▶ 1¹/₂ yards (1.4m) heavyweight interfacing or buckram

## What To Do

**1** Begin by cutting pieces from Christmas-print tablecloth: two 17¹/₂ x 14 inches (44.5 x 36cm) for front and back, two 4¹/₄ x 14 inches (11 x 36) for sides, one 17¹/₂ x 4¹/₄ inches (44.5 x 11cm) for bottom, and two 3 x 15 inches (7.5 x 38cm) for handles. Measurements include ¹/₂-inch (13mm) seam allowances. From jacquard tablecloth, cut same-size pieces for lining. Cut fusible batting for each tablecloth piece, but ¹/₂ inch (13mm) smaller all around.

**2** Centering, fuse batting to wrong side of corresponding printed tablecloth pieces. Baste interfacing to wrong side of front and back lining pieces.

**3** To assemble, pin printed tablecloth front, bottom, and back pieces together with right sides facing and edges even. Seam along long edges, with ¹/₂-inch (13mm) seam allowances. With right sides facing, pin joined front/bottom/back around side pieces, matching edges and placing seams at corners. Stitch all around; clip into seam allowance at corners. Turn top edges ¹/₂ inch (13mm) to wrong side and press.

**4** Assemble jacquard lining in the same manner, but trim ¹/₂ inch (13mm) from top edges of interfacing before turning top edges of fabric to wrong side. Topstitch along top edge. Insert lining into bag, wrong sides together and seams matching. Pin along top edge.

**5** For handles, fuse batting to center of lining on the wrong side. Fold long edges of each printed tablecloth and lining piece ¹/₂ inch (13mm) to wrong side and press. Pin printed tablecloth handle and lining together with wrong sides facing; topstitch all around. Insert ends of handles between lining and printed tablecloth bag, 6 inches (15cm) from side seams. Topstitch through all layers at base of handles. Slipstitch lining in place all around top edge of bag.

# Tablecloth Teddy

**Size:** 21 inches (53.5cm) tall

## What You'll Need

▶ Cotton jacquard tablecloth, approximately 1 square yard (100cm)
▶ Cotton print napkin or tablecloth scrap (ours is left over from making a stocking) in contrasting print for bow tie
▶ Sewing thread to match
▶ Polyester fiberfill for stuffing
▶ Scrap of black felt for nose
▶ 2 buttons, ⁵/₈ inch (16mm) in diameter for eyes
▶ Small amount of six-strand embroidery floss, for mouth

## What To Do

**1** Refer to the directions and patterns for the Patchwork Teddy Bear in the Quilts chapter, pages 59-60, using a tablecloth for the pieces. Notice that this bear's mouth curves into a smile.

**2** To make a bow tie, cut a 7 x 6¹/₂-inch (18 x 16.5cm) rectangle and a 1⁵/₈ x 3-inch (4.5 x 8cm) strip from tablecloth scrap. Fold the rectangle lengthwise in half, right side in, and stitch along one long side and one short side, ¹/₂ inch (13mm) from edges. Clip corners and turn to right side. Turn open edges to inside and slipstitch closed; press. Also press long edges of strip ¹/₂ inch (13mm) to wrong side. Pinch center of rectangle and wrap tightly with strip; stitch to secure and to attach to bear's neck.

# Christmas Stockings

**Sizes: Large,** 18 inches (46cm); **Medium,** 15 inches (38cm)

## What You'll Need for Each

▶ Christmas-print tablecloth and or towels (These were made from sections of 2 Christmas-print tablecloths.)

▶ Coordinating fabric for lining, 12 x 38 inches (31 x 96.5cm)

▶ Sewing thread to match fabrics

▶ Fusible batting

## What To Do

1 Enlarge pattern for the medium or large stocking at right. *Solid lines on these patterns represent stitching lines.* Before cutting out pattern, add ¹/₂ inch (13mm) all around for seam allowances.

2 For stocking front, pin pattern to cloth and cut out. Reverse the pattern to cut a mirror image for the back. For lining, cut a same-size front and back from coordinating fabric. Cut a front and back from fusible batting, but omit seam allowances. Center batting on wrong side of lining pieces, and iron to fuse.

3 To assemble the stocking, pin tablecloth pieces together with right sides facing and edges even. Sew all around, using ¹/₂-inch (13mm) seam allowances and leaving top edge open. Repeat for lining. Clip into seam allowances around curves. Turn stocking right side out and set aside.

4 To make cuffs, cut rectangles from tablecloth using a finished edge for one long side. Use finished edge for bottom of cuff. For flat cuff on large stocking, cut a 8 ¹/₂ x 17-inch (22 x 43cm) rectangle. Fold in half, lengthwise, and position at top of stocking with ¹/₂ inch (13mm) of remaining long edge folded to inside of stocking. Seam short sides closed to line up with stocking seam on heel side. Pin in place. For ruffled cuff on medium stocking, cut a

4 x 34-inch (10 x 86.5cm) rectangle: Gather top edge of ruffle with small gathering stitches, position on stocking as per flat cuff.

5 To make a hanging loop, cut a 2 x 5-inch (5 x 13cm) strip from a finished edge of tablecloth (or towel) remnant and fold lengthwise in half, wrong sides together. Fold crosswise in half and baste ends securely to stocking front at top of stocking above heel with loop facing in.

6 To assemble stocking, insert lining into stocking, matching up toes and seams. Turn raw edges under and sew around top edges through front, cuff, and lining.

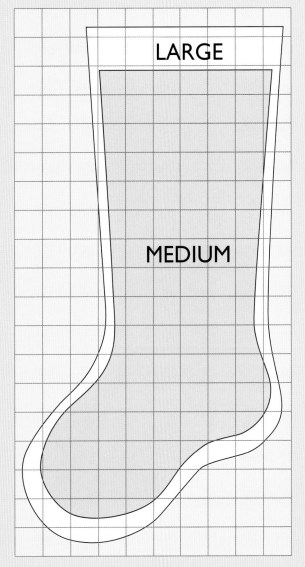

**REDUCED PATTERNS FOR STOCKINGS**
Each square equals 1 inch (2.5cm).

# Chapter Seven

*Doilies*

The word "doily" conjures up snowflakelike images of exquisitely detailed lacy circles. Whether forgotten family treasures or thrift-shop buys, these remnants of the past are finding a place in the present. Exploring the variety of shapes and textures can bring rewarding results.

Look closely at
Rosemary Drysdale's
beautifully designed
pastel pillows. The entire
surface of each flanged
top is layered with
doilies that she has dyed
(a few ecru doilies are
the exception) and
stitched together.

Everyday garden-variety clay pots get an
entirely new look with the addition of a few
doilies. Select doily colors to match your
plants or vice versa. These pots look pretty
lined up on a window sill all year-round.

Reminiscent of Victorian parlors and found tucked away in attic trunks and bureau drawers, these dainty stitcheries are coming out of closets everywhere and appearing on designer clothes and contemporary home accessories.

Created as decorative protection under place settings, lamps, bowls, and vases, these nostalgic patterns still have great appeal. Handmade by the thousands and designed not only to lie flat on a table but to withstand repeated launderings, there is still a great abundance of them.

### A LITTLE HISTORY

History credits the word "doily" to a 17th-century draper in London named Mr. Doily (or Doyley) who introduced antimacassars, also known as "tidies," to home decor. These doilies were created in sets of three to protect upholstered furniture. There was one for the back of the chair or sofa to safeguard against "Macassar," the men's hair pomade of the time, and then a doily for each arm. As many of us still remember from visits to our grandmothers' homes, these doilies used on chairs were seldom round;

the one on the back of the chair was larger and often elongated and the ones on the arms were smaller versions in the same fabric or pattern.

The transition from these antimacassars to the doilies used for place settings is not entirely clear except that many of the same needlework techniques were used and the idea of using these creations to protect a surface remains constant.

Doilies used on dining tables became stylish in America after the middle of the 19th century, flourished in Victorian times, and remained popular through the 1950s and into the 1960s. Part of their appeal may have been that these were projects that could be completed fairly quickly and that there was a great variety of designs, techniques, and uses to choose from. At first doilies were used, instead of a tablecloth, just for tea or for breakfast, but soon it was acceptable to set a table with them at lunchtime.

Made for specific purposes, doilies come in many different sizes and shapes. The bare minimum for a place setting would be three: one to fit under the plate, another for the bread-and-butter dish and another for the tumbler or goblet. But few hostesses stopped there: Doilies were made to fit under every serving piece and platter as well as finger bowls; bouillon bowls; rose bowls; celery, olive, and bread dishes; tea cups; and just about any other use that came to mind. Sizes for place-setting doilies vary from 4 inches (10cm) for coasters to 8 or 9 inches (20 to 23cm) for a bread-and-butter or dessert plate to 10 inches (25cm) for a luncheon plate. Those for serving pieces, platters, hot pads (used over asbestos), centerpieces, trays, and table lamps depended on the size required. Often, doilies will have a word describing their use as part of the design, such as "Bread" or "Hot Rolls" or "Ice Water" crocheted or embroidered into the doily.

If you stop for a moment and speculate that if a woman made six doilies for each place setting, served six friends and/or family members for lunch, and then count the extra pieces for serving plates, etc., it's soon clear why such a quantity of them were made. And, of course, no one had just one set. There were plainer doilies for family

**Make a memory by combining a few of your favorite things. This collage fits an antique frame and includes a section of a flower doily, two coaster-size doilies, and some nostalgic paper cutouts.**

use, fancy ones for special events, and even some with seasonal or holiday themes. Multiply that number by a neighborhood, or a town!

There are some standard patterns that you will learn to recognize including—in knit and/or crochet—pinecone, star, forget-me-not, spider web, pineapple, diamond, and the heavier-weight popcorn stitch: They look pretty much as the names suggest. However, there are many variations within these patterns as women added their personal touches. For example, the April 1929 issue of *Needlecraft Magazine* published directions for "Mrs. E. Roetger's Knitted Doily With Star Center," which showed an 8-pointed star not unlike a starfish, and there was also "Mary Card's Five-Leaved Doily in Filet Crochet," which was challenging in its complexity. An interesting side note is that an ad appearing in this same issue, next to the delicate handwork patterns, was for 20 Mule Team Borax and read: "For linen pieces—dainty fabrics of any kind—you can wash them with Borax safer than anything else. Use your favorite laundry soap but use 20 Mule Team Borax with it for best results. Borax gets white things really white, makes the laundry work easier—and is absolutely harmless."

A trio of flower doilies are a pretty touch in a bedroom. The smaller pillow features a pansy pattern that alternates shades of purple and of yellow blossoms. Roses are also a favorite motif, as shown on the two larger pillows below.

## DIFFERENCES IN DOILIES

We usually think of doilies as being *crocheted*, and the majority that you'll find at flea markets will probably fit this category: Among the possible reasons why crocheting was especially popular were ads like this one in 1938: "Do it [crochet] when you are listening to the radio or when a friend drops in for a chat. Crocheting occupies your hands and yet becomes so automatic you can talk and listen and crochet—and it all goes so smoothly together!" Hard to believe, but in 1957 E. Hiddleson of Vallejo, California, offered an instruction book for "10 doilies and chair sets never before seen in print": By this time, perhaps women could watch television while crocheting.

However, crochet is just one of many techniques used for making doilies. There are *embroidered* doilies, usually white-on-white and some with eyelet work.

Early in this century, pale-colored silk threads were used to embroider flowers and fruit on doilies (especially violets, strawberries, and grapes). Motifs from favorite china patterns were adapted to embroidery: Bright colors were considered garish but the blue-and-white and pastel colors worked very well. One thread company even developed a pattern that reflected the open latticework design of milk glass to be used with, what else, milk glass dishes.

Doilies are not always round or oval. There are fine examples of *drawn thread* doilies that are square: Worked on linen, threads were removed and restitched to create rows of openwork patterns. The more rows of openwork, the more valuable the doily.

*Battenberg* (a form of braided lace developed in America) doilies are frequently irregular in shape because of the comparatively large curvilinear designs that result from this technique. They are very beautiful: Often, Battenberg lace is used as a border on a linen center.

You will also find delicate *tatted* doilies consisting of small repetitive looped stitches: *cutwork* doilies, which are a form of openwork and embroidery and are usually white-on-white with scalloped edges; and hairpin lace doilies. *Hairpin lace* doilies are very airy and cobweblike;

This aqua green comforter is a sampler of many different kinds of doilies. One or more doily is appliquéd to each of the squares. And the squares themselves are damask dinner napkins purchased at a flea market. For a larger-size spread, just add more napkins and more doilies.

in the 1940s, however, hairpin lace doilies were stitched in heavier crochet cottons and bright colors (shades of pink and green were favored) and then stiffly starched.

It's not at all unusual to find doilies that combine several of these needlework techniques. In fact, almost, any suitably sized decorative handwork that was intended to go under something else can be considered a doily.

## FLOWER DOILIES

These doilies feature a border—and sometimes a center—of colorful flowers. Especially popular in the 1940s, flowers became brighter and bolder after the war. Variegated threads were used to crochet the flowers and choices included roses in all sizes and colors; pansies, combining solid purples and yellows with variegated lavender threads; yellow and white daisies; blue forget-me-nots with yellow centers and often in double or triple rows; green-and-white pond lilies; "passion flowers"; and daffodils. Many of the flowers were three-dimensional and some edges had a ruffled effect as well. Magazines published "recipes" for making the stiffest ruffles, varying the mixture of starch and sometimes substituting such household basics as sugar and water.

**What could be simpler, or prettier, than a starched doily threaded with ribbon and filled with flowers? Top and bottom center doilies are good examples of cutwork. The doily at left is all crochet and the one at right features a crocheted border.**

The wide selection of color in these doilies makes them a practical decorating accessory: You'll be able to select from pastel pinks to endless shades of purple to bright reds, yellows, and oranges. Often green is incorporated into the design for leaves or other accents. As you'll see, we used these flower doilies on a number of different projects, from pillows to a flowerpot.

## SHOPPING FOR DOILIES

Although originally intended for entertaining and made in matching sets, individual doilies are what you will most likely discover these days. (An exception might be a smaller set of coaster-size doilies.) However, it's not important that they match up. The fun of collecting doilies is to realize just how many varieties there really are.

Pay attention to condition. If there are stains, these are probably old stains from food or wine and are not likely to come out. If it's noticeable that different types of thread have been used either for mending purposes or because the original was made from leftover bits and pieces, pass it by. When laundered, these different threads will become even more apparent.

Some imperfect doilies do have many options. We dyed some doilies for the pretty pastel pillows and used just a section of a doily for the framed collage. Scraps of white and ecru doilies were used on the handsome wreath ornaments. Sometimes, you will be fortunate enough to buy torn or damaged doilies for just $2 or $3 apiece.

Crocheted doilies are the most reasonably priced as there are more of them. Cost depends on the size, condition, and intricacy of the work. A 6- or 7-inch (15 or 18cm) crocheted doily costs between $4 and $11.

Smaller doilies are not necessarily less and larger doilies will definitely be more, as much as $25 for a handsome and intricately knit or crocheted doily. Doilies with words such as "Bread" will cost $16 to $24. Unusual sayings will be more than that. Prices are higher in areas where there is a revival of interest in Victorian houses and decorating, as doilies are authentically used and the demand is greater.

Embroidered, drawn-thread, cutwork, and

A man's vest, purchased at a thrift shop, is now suited for a woman. All it took was one large doily cut in half for the lapels and two smaller doilies for each pocket. Vintage jewelry—in this case a brooch, a broken bracelet, and a single earring—is optional.

These Victorian-style ornaments are sections of fabric and doilies tucked into scored Styrofoam balls. The bow on the wreath is also made from doilies. Doily-trimmed ornaments could decorate a tree or garland.

Battenberg doilies may well start at $12 to $15, and if there are several different techniques, such as an embroidered center with a Battenberg or drawn-thread border, the cost will be higher. There are some reproduction doilies—especially Battenberg—on the market: Made in China, these aren't much less expensive; if you handle them, they will feel a little stiffer because they are new and they may also have labels noting the country of origin.

Flower doilies range in price from $12 to $24. You may find a matching set of serving-size flower doilies and, if so, a set of three or more pieces can be $40. I still see some sets of four of the 1940s pink and green hairpin lace doilies for $24 a set. I have the feeling that these were made and given as gifts but seldom used because they afforded very little protection to the table.

## TIPS TO REMEMBER

Like all of us, you may get confused between table doilies and anti-macassars and tray covers. One guideline is that chair backs often have specific designs worked into them, often using filet crochet. Therefore, if you see an irregular shape (flat across the top, for example) with butterflies, flowers, peacocks, or other recognizable symbols, dates, or monograms, it's probably a chair-back cover. If it's an even rectangle, it's more likely that it was made to fit a serving tray. Arm and chair-back doilies are also made in shapes such as vases of flowers. But to confuse the issue further, there are also novelty doilies that are crocheted in the shapes of teapots and flowers as well.

There is some debate between experts about "centerpieces" and doilies: Some say that after 12 or 14 inches (30 or 35cm) in diameter, a doily becomes a centerpiece. However, the September 1957 issue of *Workbasket* magazine described an "exquisite filet doily that measures about 38½ inches in diameter when completed." Most people would consider this a little large for a typical doily. Centerpieces are also referred to as a "between meal," which simply meant that in between meals, after all the silver, china, and linens had been cleared away, the table wouldn't look bare and would have a decorative fabric placed on it. I have a collection of framed doilies the largest of which is an intricate cutwork and embroidered oval 18 by 27 inches (46 x 68cm), and the smallest is a drawn-thread coaster 4 by 4 inches (10cm x 10cm).

For the purposes shown here, simply buy whatever size or shape doily will fit your project. Noted California designer and author Jean Ray Laury was one of the first to incorporate vintage doilies into her prize-winning quilts and wall hangings—over 25 years ago—and she remains the inspiration for the rest of us. Jean cut doilies into flower, heart, and bird shapes and appliquéd them to felt and velvet and used small doilies for halos on angelic figures. Her motive? "They deserve to be preserved." When it comes to

choosing background fabrics, Jean advises: "If your needlework is in ecru or naturals, a warm color such as a deeper beige, cocoa-brown, rust or cinnamon may look well. But try a variety to see how each looks. Be daring and, if you need to, take the doilies directly to the fabric shop where you can place them on various colors of yardage to make your choice." White or cream-colored backgrounds can be very romantic looking combined with doilies. Imagine a simple drawstring purse for a bride made of off-white satin with a doily on the front and another on the back for "something old." Darker colors and textured fabrics such as a navy or burgundy velvet are more dramatic and more formal, and showcase the needlework to much better advantage. If you purchase stiffer doilies, they'll be easier to work with.

It's hard to imagine that in the days before computers or dishwashers or other modern conveniences, when housework was more cumbersome, women were able to find the time and patience to stitch these wonderful decorative accessories. How many of us could manage that today? What we can do is take advantage of their industriousness and enjoy the fruits of their labors in our homes with very little effort at all.

**This "Love" doily speaks for itself. It's fun to collect only doilies with words. The larger crocheted piece is either a chair-back cover or a tray cover that was made to commemorate Lindbergh's 1927 flight.**

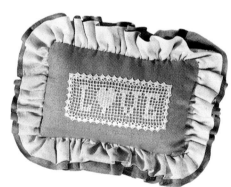

## Pretty Pastels

**Sizes: Small Pillow,** 14 inches (36cm) square, not including 2-inch (5cm) flange all around; **Large Pillow,** 18 inches (46cm) square, not including 2¹/₂-inch (6.5cm) flange all around

### What You'll Need for Each

▶ Approximately 15 doilies in assorted sizes, shapes, and textures
▶ Cold-water dyes in various pastels
▶ ³/₄ yard (.7m) white fabric for each pillow top (doilies' background), and pastel calico fabric for pillow back
▶ Sewing thread to match fabric
▶ 14- or 18-inch (36 or 46cm) square pillow forms
▶ Rubber gloves
▶ Spray starch

### What To Do

1 To dye doilies, wear rubber gloves and work in a sink or basin. Follow manufacturer's directions for preparing a dye bath. For a range of shades, leave some doilies in dye bath longer than others. Rinse doilies thoroughly and allow to dry; press flat with spray starch. *Note: A few ecru-colored doilies were not dyed.*

2 From white fabric, cut pillow top for doilies' background: a 19-inch (48.5cm) square for small pillow, or a 23-inch (58.5cm) square for large pillow. From calico fabrics, cut 2 rectangles for an overlapped back: 19 x 13 inches (48.5 x 33cm) for small pillow, or 23 x 14¹/₂ inches (58.5 x 37cm) for large pillow.

3 Arrange dyed doilies on right side of pillow top, overlapping and layering smaller doilies on top of larger ones to cover white fabric. Pin doilies in place. Some doilies may extend past edges; trim these even with pillow-top edges. Slipstitch doilies in place around unconcealed doily edges; then straight-stitch, or zigzag-stitch by machine, outside doilies close to pillow-top edges all around.

4 To make an overlapped back, hem one long edge on each calico rectangle and overlap them so they form a square the same size as the pillow top.

5 To assemble, lay pillow top on pinned-together pillow-back pieces, right sides facing. Stitch all around, ¹/₂ inch (13mm) from edges. Clip into the seam allowances at corners, and turn to right side through back opening. Press.

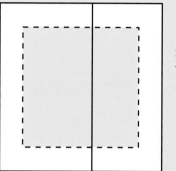

DIAGRAM FOR SEWING THE FLANGE

6 To create the flange, refer to the diagram above and stitch around—2 inches (5cm) for small pillow or 2¹/₂ inches (6.5cm) for large pillow—from the outside edges, sewing through all layers. Insert pillow form into center through the back opening.

## Flowerpots

**Size:** As shown: 3¹/₄ and 7¹/₂ inches (8.5 and 19cm) tall

### What You'll Need

▶ Doilies in various sizes
▶ Terra-cotta clay pots in desired sizes
▶ White glue
▶ Fabric stiffener (optional)
▶ ⁵/₈ yard (.6m) twisted cord or amount to fit around pot
▶ Foam paintbrush

## What To Do

1 Glue one or more doilies to sides of each flowerpot, as shown in the photograph. The large pot on the left features three 6-inch (15.5cm) round doilies, slightly overlapping; the small pot features a 3½-inch (9cm) doily with a contrast-color center and edging, which hugs the rim; and the pot on the right has a 14-inch (36cm) round doily with pink roses folded off-center so as to show all the flowers, glued with folded edge close to rim. Allow glue to dry.

2 Glue cord around top of pot, just below rim, overlapping ends of cord.

3 To waterproof doilies and cord, use fabric stiffener or dilute white glue with a little water to the consistency of heavy cream. Apply with foam brush over each doily and to twisted cord. Allow to dry.

## Doily Collage

**Size:** As desired

## What You'll Need

▶ Assorted doilies: one 6-inch (15.5cm) round doily with a crocheted floral edge and two 3-inch (8cm) doilies were used here

▶ Frame of your choice: as shown, this 3-inch (8cm) wide frame surrounds a 7 x 9½-inch (18 x 24.5cm) oval window opening

▶ Cardboard to fit inside dimensions of frame

▶ Small amount of pale blue taffeta to cover cardboard

▶ Assorted nostalgic or botanical paper cutouts; shown here are a gloved hand and a butterfly

▶ Glue stick

▶ Pencil or dressmaker's marking pencil

## What To Do

1 Remove backing and glass from frame. Trace around existing backing on cardboard. If frame is without a backing, place frame on cardboard and trace around inside opening of frame. Cut out cardboard for collage background.

2 To cover cardboard with fabric, place cardboard for background on wrong side of fabric and trace around with pencil. Cut fabric 1 inch (2.5cm) larger all around. Reposition cardboard on fabric as before, and clip into fabric that extends beyond edges, every few inches, forming tabs. Apply glue to edges of cardboard in back. Fold tabs to the back and press into the glue to secure.

3 Arrange doilies and cutouts until you are pleased with the composition. Position largest, flower-edged doily first, then layer smaller items on top and around it. Secure all items in place with glue. Note that one leaf motif on large doily was left loose, temporarily, so that butterfly cutout could be glued down partially underneath the doily. Trim pieces even with edges of background as necessary.

4 Clean glass and reinsert in frame. Insert collage in frame and replace backing securely.

## Flower Ring Pillows

**Sizes:** **Small Pillow,** 12 inches (30.5cm) in diameter; **Large Pillows,** 18 inches (46cm) in diameter; all, 2½ inches (6.5cm) deep

## What You'll Need for Each

▶ Round crocheted doily with flower border, a little smaller than desired pillow

▶ Medium-weight cotton or linen fabric in a color to coordinate with doily: ¾ yard (.7m) for small pillow, 1 yard (1m) for large pillow

▶ Sewing thread to match fabric and doily

- Polyester fiberfill for stuffing
- Cotton cording for piping, $^1/_4$ inch (6mm) in diameter: $1^1/_8$ yards (1m) for small pillow, $1^1/_2$ yards (1.4m) for large pillow
- Compass, yardstick, straight pins

## What To Do

1 To cut fabric pieces, use a yardstick and compass as appropriate, and work in the following order: first, 1 boxing strip along grain of fabric; second, 2 circles for pillow top and back; and then, from remaining fabric, $1^3/_4$-inch (4.5cm) wide strips cut on the bias for piping. For small pillow, make boxing strip $3^1/_4$ x $38^1/_2$ inches (8.5 x 98cm), circles $12^3/_4$ inches (32.5cm) in diameter, and piece bias strips to total 40 inches (102cm) for piping. For large pillow, make boxing strip $3^1/_4$ x 53 inches (8.5 x 135cm), circles 18 inches (46cm) in diameter, and piece strips to total 54 inches (137.5cm) for piping. These dimensions include $^3/_8$-inch (1cm) seam allowances.

2 Pin doily, centered, on right side of pillow top. Slipstitch all around doily to secure it in place.

3 Make fabric-covered piping, referring to the trimming how-to's of the General Directions, Chapter Eight. Apply it around pillow top.

4 Assemble pillow, following pillow-making how-to's for a box pillow in the General Directions.

# Napkin-and-Doily Comforter

**Size:** $55^1/_2$ x 74 inches (141 x 188cm)

## What You'll Need

- Assortment of white and ecru doilies: 27 were used here, in sizes ranging from 5 to 14 inches (13 to 36cm) round and square

- 12 damask napkins, here 19 inches (48.5cm) square, in aqua
- Twin-size high-loft quilt batting
- Twin-size sheet for comforter backing
- 5 yards (5m) $^1/_8$-inch (3mm) wide ecru satin ribbon, for tie-quilting comforter
- Large-eyed embroidery needle, straight pins

## What To Do

1 For comforter top, remove hems from napkins and press seams out flat. Pin 1 large or several smaller, overlapping doilies to each damask napkin. Slipstitch around all unconcealed edges to secure doilies in place.

2 To assemble comforter top, arrange napkins in 3 rows of 4, varying the size and shade of doilies. Working in pairs, begin by pinning napkins together along one side, with right sides facing, matching edges. Use $^1/_4$-inch (6mm) seam allowances throughout. Machine-sew napkins together along pinned edge, then unfold and return to the original arrangement. Repeat to join 5 more pairs of napkins. Then, continuing in the same manner, join 2 pairs of napkins to form each row of 4 napkins. Press seams open. Stitch rows together, with right sides facing, edges even, and seams matching. Press seams open.

3 Cut batting and backing to same size as comforter top. Spread backing right side up on batting, with comforter top right side down over backing. Smooth layers, and pin to secure. Stitch around, leaving a 10-inch (25.5cm) opening. Clip across seam allowances at corners, and turn right side out. Turn open edges to inside and slipstitch closed. Press edges flat, then topstitch all around twice, first $^1/_4$ inch (6mm) and then $^3/_4$ inch (2cm) from edges.

4 To tie-quilt the comforter, cut ribbon into twenty 9-inch (23cm) lengths, cutting ends at an angle. Thread one strand in needle. Start at the center of the comforter and work outward all around as follows: At an intersection of napkins, bring needle down to the backing, then back up to the comforter top, $^1/_8$ inch (3mm) away. Remove needle and tie ribbon ends in a square knot, then in a bow. Repeat at each intersection of napkins, and at each seam along inside row of topstitches. Reinforce each bow knot with a couple of stitches to hold in place.

# Wall Pockets

**Sizes:** 6 to 8 inches (15.5 to 20.5cm) high

## What You'll Need for Each

▶ Round doily, as shown, 6 to 8 inches (15.5 to 20.5cm) in diameter
▶ Fabric stiffener or white glue
▶ 2 or more various-colored ribbons: $5/8$ yard (.6m) each, $1/16$ or $3/8$ inch (2mm or 1cm) wide
▶ Small bunch of dried flowers
▶ Styrofoam® plastic foam cone
▶ Masking tape
▶ Cellophane wrap

## What To Do

1 Cover cone with cellophane wrap. Also cover table surface with cellophane wrap.

2 To stiffen doily, use fabric stiffener or white glue diluted with a little water to the consistency of heavy cream. Mix glue or pour stiffener in a bowl, then immerse doily. Squeeze doily between your fingers to remove most of the liquid. Wrap doily around the cone, beginning at the point and overlapping doily edges. Place on covered tabletop with overlapped edges face down. Allow to dry thoroughly.

3 To finish, remove cone. Thread ribbon through openwork holes of both layers of doily at overlap, as shown in photo. Tie ribbon ends together and make a simple bow. Use openwork on the back to hang wall pocket from a nail or picture hanger. Fill pocket with dried flowers.

# Vintage Vest

**Size:** As desired

## What You'll Need

▶ Purchased vest: a man's vest from a 3-piece suit was used here
▶ Round doilies: one 12 inches (30.5cm) in diameter, two 5 inches (13cm) in diameter
▶ Sewing thread to match doilies
▶ Vintage jewelry, which may be broken or antique-look jewelry: shown here, brooch, broken bracelet, an earring missing its mate

## What To Do

1 For lapels, cut large doily in half. Arrange half of doily along center front opening on each side, with cut edges folded to the inside and top of doily covering shoulder seam. Pin in place, then slipstitch doily halves to vest along all edges, using thread to match doily.

2 Pin a small doily along each pocket, folding doily over pocket edge to inside. Slipstitch in place along all edges.

3 Arrange jewelry on doilies where desired. Attach as appropriate, taking care to work through the vest as well as the doily when attaching jewelry. The brooch is pinned to the lapel. The back of the single earring was pried off with pliers, and then the earring was stitched in place, with thread wrapping its narrow areas. The broken bracelet was draped around the curve of a doily and stitched with thread around its links and eye ring. (Jewelry can also be attached with a glue gun.)

# Wreath Ornaments

**Size:** 24 inches (61cm) in diameter

## What You'll Need

▶ Approximately 15 assorted doilies

▶ Eight 4-inch (10.5cm) Styrofoam® plastic foam balls

▶ $1/2$ yard (.5m) medium-weight blue cotton fabric

▶ 24-inch (61cm) artificial green wreath

▶ White glue

▶ Rubber bands

▶ Small piece of malleable wire

▶ Large rectangular doily, small doily or medallion, and fabric stiffener for bow

▶ Blunt knife, such as a butter knife or small putty knife, to make indentations in plastic foam

▶ Small, sharp scissors

▶ Dried hydrangea blossoms

▶ Glue gun and glue sticks

## What To Do

1 Cover each of the Styrofoam balls with fabric, using the quick-tuck method as follows: Begin by marking off 4 equal divisions on each ball, by wrapping 2 rubber bands around the widest part of the ball at right angles to each other. Draw a sharp pencil along the edge of the rubber bands to make indentations defining the edges of the 4 equal divisions, then remove the rubber bands.

2 Use pattern to cut out 4 sections of fabric for each ball. To attach fabric section to the ball, center 1 piece of fabric on top of lines drawn for 1 quarter section. You should be able to feel the indented groove made in the surface of the Styrofoam through the fabric. Place blade of a blunt knife on the fabric where you can feel the groove, and push fabric down into the Styrofoam at a 90-degree angle for about $1/4$ inch (6mm). Referring to the diagram on page 129, push the fabric into ball all along the groove. Smooth out any puckers by running blade along tuck line from top to

## ACTUAL-SIZE PATTERN FOR FABRIC SECTION

bottom of ball. Use a pair of small scissors to trim away any fabric that protrudes. Continue to tuck in the fabric for each section until ball is covered.

3 Attach pieces of doily to the balls: Tuck doily edges into grooves where convenient; otherwise use white glue to adhere in place. Continue until each quarter section is covered. Hot-glue decorated balls to wreath.

4 To create a bow: Immerse large doily and small doily, or medallion, into fabric stiffener or white glue thinned with water to the consistency of heavy cream. Squeeze doilies between your

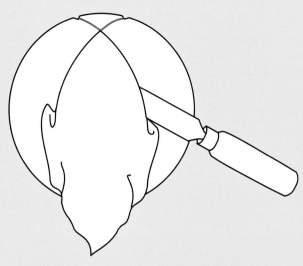

DIAGRAM FOR QUICK-TUCK METHOD

fingers to remove most of the liquid. Pinch center of large doily and wrap with wire, leaving wire ends long. Lay wet items on cellophane wrap and let dry. Glue small doily or medallion to pinched area, for bowknot, and attach to wreath between ornaments, wrapping wire ends securely in place.

5 Finish trimming wreath by adding small bunches of dried hydrangea blossoms between balls; hot-glue in place if necessary.

# Filet Crochet Pillows

**Sizes:** **Small Pillow**, 12 x 8 inches (30.5 x 20.5cm), not including two 2³/₄-inch (7cm) ruffles all around;
**Large Pillow**, 21 x 16¹/₂ inches (53.5 x 42cm), not including two 3¹/₂-inch (9cm) ruffles all around, to fit a standard bed pillow

## What You'll Need

▶ Rectangular filet crochet doily: 7¹/₂ x 3¹/₂-inch (19 x 9cm) doily shown on small pillow; 17¹/₂ x 13-inch (44.5 x 33cm) doily shown on large pillow

▶ Medium-weight cotton or linen fabrics 44-inches wide (1.2m): for small pillow, ¹/₂ yard (.5m) dark gray and 1¹/₄ yard (1.3m) pale gray; for large pillow, 1 yard (1m) blue, ¹/₂ yard (.5m) ecru

▶ Sewing thread to match doilies and fabrics

▶ Polyester fiberfill for stuffing, or bed pillow, if appropriate

## What To Do

1 For pillow top, measure the doily and cut a rectangle from darker fabric 3 inches (8cm) larger all around. This includes ¹/₂-inch (13mm) seam allowances. Cut a same-size piece for a back.

2 Pin doily, centered, on right side of pillow top. Slipstitch all around doily to secure in place.

3 To make each of the hemmed ruffles that form a double ruffle, add the measurements of all 4 sides of your pillow top and multiply by 2 to obtain the necessary length. From remaining dark fabric, cut 4¹/₂-inch (11.5cm) wide strips along the grain, and piece them to total the length measurement obtained. For the contrast ruffle, use light-colored fabric to cut 4-inch (10.5cm) wide strips and piece to total the same length as before. Follow trimming how-to's of the General Directions, Chapter Eight, and make 2 hemmed ruffles. However, after joining ends and hemming 1 long edge of each strip, pin them together with right sides up and raw edges matching, gathering raw edges of both layers at the same time. Pin and baste to pillow top.

4 To make a closed-back pillow, place pillow top on back with right sides facing. Stitch around 3 sides and corners of the fourth, slightly to the inside of basting stitches. Clip seam allowances at corners, and turn to right side. Insert pillow form or stuffing, turn open edges to inside, and slipstitch closed.

5 To use with a bed pillow, make an overlapped back according to the pillow-making section of the General Directions, Chapter Eight.

# General Directions

Step-by-step directions for each of the projects shown have been given in previous chapters. However, it's handy to have a reference guide to learn—or simply review—basic procedures. Here are the most frequently used techniques in this book as well as helpful hints on working with vintage fabrics.

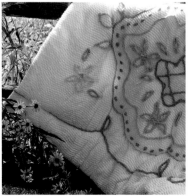

*F*irst of all, assemble your flea-market purchases. Spread them out carefully and consider how you plan to use them. Inspect textiles for worn spots, stains, yellowed crease marks, and tears. Even items that appear never to have been used should probably be laundered before you work with them to remove foldlines and mildew, and to insure preshrinking. Doilies that have already been sized or starched are an exception as you don't want to remove the stiffening.

## EMBROIDERED LINENS

Most embroidered linens are stitched with color-fast threads, but check a small section to be certain. As the stitching goes through to the back side, you can take a clean white cloth, dampen it in cold water, and rub it gently across the threads on the wrong side to see if any color comes off on the cloth. If the cloth remains white, try again with warm water and a little detergent. It may be that these linens were completed or repaired with different threads, and for that reason it's wise to test more than one area.

Once you've established that the threads are colorfast, towels, pillowcases, napkins, and many runners can be machine-washed on a gentle cycle but I would not put them in the dryer. Remove and press while still damp. Use spray starch when pressing linens to provide extra body.

Many textile dealers prefer Ultra-Biz® for removing stains and fold marks. Others suggest making a paste of Cascade® dishwasher detergent and water and applying it to stubborn spots before laundering or adding a little white vinegar with the detergent. Snowy® bleach, a small amount of Clorox 2®, and a weak solution of Wisk® on stubborn spots have also been recommended to me. However, without knowing the cause of the original marks, there's no guarantee that they will completely disappear.

Exceptions to machine laundering include runners that are of sheer or fragile material and textiles with deep crocheted or delicately fringed edgings. Smaller items such as the fringed coasters used on the Christening dress should also be washed by hand in mild detergent.

## CHENILLE

Chenille bedspreads actually benefit from machine washing and drying. The colors brighten and the tufts fluff up. Wash separately with your regular detergent and a small amount of Clorox 2® if desired. Be sure to launder chenille before purchasing any matching or coordinating trims as the bedspread colors can change.

## QUILTS

Antique quilts should be cleaned by experts, if at all. The quilts used in these projects are mostly from the 1930s through the 1950s and are already damaged in some way. But use care when laundering quilt sections as they are comprised of many pieces and can easily come apart—particularly if they're hand-stitched.

For mounted quilt blocks additional cleaning is probably not necessary although cotton blocks can be gently hand-washed in lukewarm water with mild soap. For duffel bags and totes a fairly clean quilt section that has been thoroughly aired should be adequate. Unfinished quilt tops have seldom been used and may be fine as is. If there is an odor of moth balls or mustiness and the top is securely machine-stitched, you can dip it into cold or lukewarm water in a bathtub with a little detergent and rinse thoroughly; do not wring. It is best to spread them out flat to dry because hanging wet quilt tops will place too much stress on the many seams.

If you must launder a quilt or quilt section that has batting in it—to use as a garment or a toy—restoration expert Camille Cognac advises, "Use your washing machine as a basin and soak the quilt (or quilt section). Spin gently, in the washing machine, to remove excess water as the weight of the water on a quilt with batting can cause the fibers to break down. Do not put it in the dryer."

You can also take a machine-stitched quilt made from colorfast fabrics (that is not a prized heirloom but one that you are planning to recycle) to a professional dry cleaner who is experienced at working with handmade and vintage fabrics.

Never try to launder a quilt piece with silk, taffeta, velvets, or intricate embroidery.

When using patchwork quilt remnants to make a project, you are cutting across a number of seams that hold the pieces together. Therefore, it is a good idea to reinforce the back (especially with quilt tops) with a fusible backing before starting. We used Pellon® Wonder Under® products. Choose the one that's appropriate for your project. A heavy-duty web is a good interfacing for a tote bag that will get a lot of wear and a lighter-weight fusible web or fleece provides a softer backing for a toy. Follow the manufacturer's directions and test on a scrap or corner first.

## LACE TRIMS AND DOILIES

Delicate lace trims and doilies are not easy to launder as they can become flimsy and difficult to work with. It's also a nuisance to iron lots of small pieces and narrow strips. Heavier cotton laces and crocheted doilies will stand up to laundering and moderate bleaching. If you are reluctant to use a commercial bleach, try rinsing in fresh lemon juice and water and drying in the sun or gently dab with equal parts hydrogen peroxide and water. Before washing a doily, it's a good idea to make a pattern by placing it on a clean piece of white paper, brown wrapping paper, or even freezer paper and marking the outline with a pencil. You'll use this outline later to block the doily back into shape.

Hand-wash laces and doilies in a sink or basin with a mild detergent. Do not leave them immersed in soap and water for more than fifteen minutes at a time. Rinse and repeat washings if necessary until the rinse water runs clear. Dry flat, pinned to a clean Turkish towel. For doilies, place your paper pattern on top of the towel. For lace trims, use a ruler or yardstick to line and pin the straight edges. Then use additional rustproof straight pins to extend and pin all the points of the lace or doily in place. When dry, press on the wrong side, with heavy-duty spray starch, on a warm setting for cottons and on a cool setting for synthetics.

If you're going to dye laces and doilies as for the Lace-Trimmed Lamp Shades or the Pretty Pastels Pillows, place them in a cold dyebath after the final rinse and when they are still damp. Cottons will absorb the dyes faster than synthetics or net laces.

To check the color, remove the lace or doily after five minutes and rinse under cold water. If it is not dark enough, return to the dyebath and check again after another five minutes until the desired color is achieved. You can always make it darker, but once it's too dark, you can't make it lighter. Rosemary Drysdale, who designed these projects, uses wooden chopsticks to rotate the pieces in the dyebath as well as to lift them out to check color. After the desired color is achieved, rinse, dry, and press as above. You may discover some inconsistencies in crocheted doilies especially after they've been washed and dyed, a possible result of completing or repairing the crocheting with different dye lots or blends of thread that react differently to the cleaning and dying. For some reason, this seems to be more prevalent in the ecru doilies.

## HANDKERCHIEFS

Handkerchiefs can be machine-laundered (except for very lacy or delicate ones such as wedding hankies), but I prefer to wash them by hand because the agitation of the machine can affect the shape and, in most instances, you want to keep them as squared off as possible—and you don't want to lose all the sizing. Press when still damp with light spray starch. If you are washing a few at a time, they can be stored in a plastic bag in the refrigerator until ready to iron.

## KITCHEN LINENS

Kitchen linens were made to stand up to wear and tear and can be machine-washed and dried although they are easier to iron when damp.

Ultra-Biz® and Arm & Hammer® are suggested detergents, and Clorox 2® will brighten colors if necessary. If there is a tear, mend it before laundering so that the size of the tear doesn't increase in the machine.

# How To Enlarge Patterns

In many instances, no pattern is required; it's only a matter of cutting fabrics to given measurements. In some cases, a pattern is given actual size. Or there may be a pattern without a grid and the directions will tell you what percentage to enlarge the pattern, as, for example, "Enlarge at 200%." In this case, simply take it to a photocopier and enlarge accordingly.

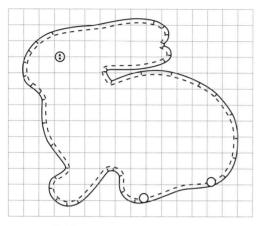

### Patterns on a Grid

A number of the patterns in this book are presented, in reduced size, on a grid. Here are two ways to convert them to the actual-size patterns you'll need:

Take the patterns to a photocopier. Refer to the scale underneath the illustration, which is usually "Each square equals 1 inch (2.5cm)," to determine how large the completed pattern should be. Then experiment with the enlarging functions on the copy machine to enlarge the pattern until each square actually does measure 1 inch (2.5cm). You may need to break the pattern down into pieces if the full pattern does not fit on one sheet of copy paper; enlarge the sections and tape them together as necessary.

To enlarge the patterns by hand, you will need a sharp lead pencil, a colored pencil, a ruler, and a large sheet of paper big enough to fit the full-size pattern. Count the number of squares in each direction and refer to the scale to determine the paper size. For example, if each square represents 1 inch (2.5cm) and there are 13 squares in one direction and 16 squares in another direction, you will need a piece of paper at least 13 x 16 inches (33 x 40.5cm) to transfer your pattern onto. Using the ruler and the colored pencil, draw a grid on the paper with the same number of squares, but make each square equal to the size indicated in the scale, i.e., 1 inch (2.5cm). Then, working square by square, from left to right and top to bottom, use a lead pencil to copy whatever design lines appear in each square of the reduced pattern onto the corresponding large square. Once you have completed this drawing, you may ignore the grid in tracing or cutting out the patterns.

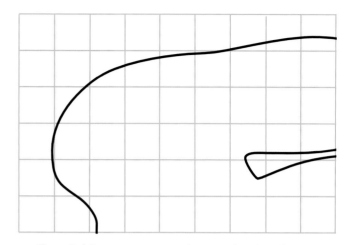

Short dash lines on a pattern indicate stitching lines. It is not necessary to copy the stitching lines or clip lines, just the outlines or cutting lines, long dash lines ("Place on fold" lines), and any 2-way arrows, which indicate how to lay the pattern out along the fabric grain or design lines. When there are several pieces, it is helpful to label what the pieces are.

### How to Complete a Half Pattern

Long dash lines on a pattern indicate that half a symmetrical pattern is provided, and the words "Place on fold" appear along the dash lines. To complete the pattern, fold a sheet of tracing paper in half. Crease it and unfold it. Place the tracing paper on top of the half pattern with the crease along the dash lines. Trace the pattern, including all markings. Fold paper on crease again and cut out the traced half pattern. Unfold the paper to produce a full pattern. Transfer any pattern markings from one half to the other if necessary. Or, if you can see the pattern details clearly through the folded tracing paper, place the *folded* paper on top of the half pattern with the fold along the dash lines. Trace the pattern and then cut out. Unfold paper as above.

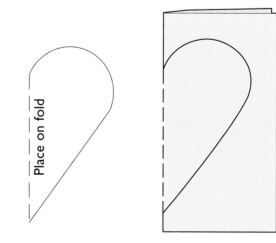

Place on fold

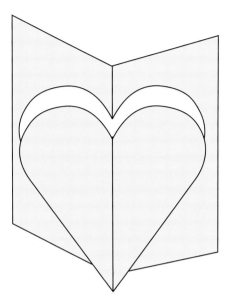

## How to Complete a Quarter Pattern

For a quarter pattern, there are perpendicular long dash lines on a pattern, such as those on the quilting pattern for the Handkerchief Tablecloth/Quilt on page 92. To complete this pattern, fold a sheet of tracing paper in half both horizontally and vertically, creasing sharply each time. Open the tracing paper, and lay it over the pattern with the creases along the long dash lines. Trace the pattern. Rotate the tracing paper, and trace the pattern onto the other three quadrants of the creased tracing paper. When each quadrant is drawn, the pattern is complete.

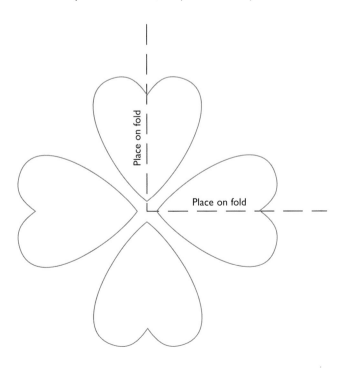

Place on fold

Place on fold

# Embroidery

The embroidery stitches in this book are used to sew details onto some of the toys. We also used embroidery around the cut edges of the Days-of-the-Week towels on the bedspread. You'll need a large-eye crewel needle or tapestry needle: Crewel needles have long eyes and sharp points. Tapestry needles have long eyes and blunter points. A crewel needle works better on most of our projects. Thread choices include embroidery floss (usually 3 or 4 of the 6 strands) and pearl cotton (which is a twisted thread). Here are the stitches we used.

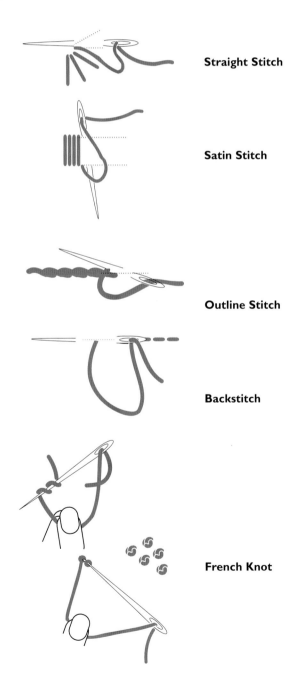

**Straight Stitch**

**Satin Stitch**

**Outline Stitch**

**Backstitch**

**French Knot**

# Sewing How-To's

Sewing by hand or machine is often a matter of personal preference. In the previous chapters, we give the methods actually used for these designs. Machine stitching is sturdier for many projects, particularly for something like a tote or duffel bag or even a toy, but if a sewing machine is not available, you can almost always hand-sew, making short running stitches, or backstitches with a double strand of thread.

## Machine Stitching

Always refer to the instructions for your sewing machine. It will suggest thread tension, pressure-foot setting, best foot, and needle for the weight of fabric you are using. It is wise to do a small test swatch to adjust these settings and features optimally. You will need a zipper foot attachment for attaching piping or zippers. Zigzag capabilities are helpful for finishing edges that tend to unravel or for gathering. Be sure to use the right-sized sewing machine needle for your project: 9 or 11 for fine fabrics, 11 or 14 for medium-weight fabrics, and 14 or 16 for heavyweight fabrics. Use the same type of thread in both the top and the bobbin.

The references to machine stitching in this book assume straight stitch, about 8 stitches to the inch or 3 stitches to the centimeter, unless otherwise indicated.

Topstitching is a visible, decorative way to sew something down, reinforce a seam, or hem. To topstitch, straight-stitch $^1\!/_8$ inch (3mm) from the edge, unless otherwise indicated.

To give a clean finish or prevent unraveling along raw edges, use a zigzag stitch or overcast stitch along these edges.

## Hand Stitching

When sewing by hand, you will want to have a sharp needle, a thimble, and a pair of small scissors for cutting threads. Select the needle size according to the weight of the fabric: The larger the number, the finer the needle, based on the thickness of the needle at the eye. Use a size 8 needle for medium-weight fabrics and a size 9 for lightweight fabrics. Choose a short needle for small stitches and fine sewing and a long needle for basting. Colored-head straight pins are easier to see; tweezers are helpful for picking out basting threads; and I find a needle threader indispensable. All-purpose, mercerized sewing thread is suggested for most projects. If your fabric is cotton, use cotton-covered polyester rather than all-synthetic thread. Use a single-strand thread about 20–22 inches (51-56cm) long (a little longer for basting) and a double thread for reinforcing areas that will be subject to extra wear and tear, as described above, as well as for sewing on buttons, snaps, and hooks and eyes.

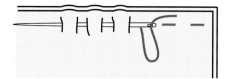

**Running Stitch**

A running stitch is used for tucks and gathering. Several stitches are held on the needle at once.

**Basting Stitch**

A basting (or tacking) stitch is used to temporarily or lightly hold two pieces of fabric together.

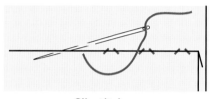

**Slipstitch**

A slipstitch secures one finished, folded, or hemmed edge to another.

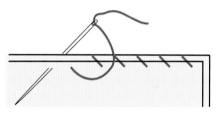

**Overcast Stitch**

This evenly-spaced diagonal stitch is used for finishing unfolded or raw edges.

## Seam Allowances

Measurements and patterns include seam allowances wherever necessary and are indicated in the directions. When joining two pieces of fabric, you'll usually pin them together with right sides facing and matching edges even. Sew pieces together, leaving the allowance between the seam and the raw edges. For example, a $^1\!/_2$-inch (13mm) seam allowance means to leave $^1\!/_2$ inch (13mm) between the seam and the edge. Press each seam as it's stitched, pressing seams open for flatter results, or to one side—usually toward the darker-color fabric for more durable results.

## How to Gather

Gathering is a method of sewing fabric in a way that allows you to gather it into soft folds. The fabric is reduced to about one third to one half its original width. For example, we used gathers on the sleeves of the pillowcase doll dresses and in the christening gown, the sundress, and on the ruffles for pillow and comforter edging.

**By Hand:** Thread the needle with a long strand of thread, and pull thread ends even to create a double strand. Knot the ends together. Make even running stitches where you wish to gather, generally close to the raw edges of the fabric. Make stitches small for tiny gathers; make larger stitches, as for basting, for fuller, larger gathers. As you stitch, you may slide the fabric toward the knot, to begin the gathering process. When you finish the line of stitching, keep the needle in place. Pull these thread ends and slide the fabric down toward the knot until the gathered fabric is the required or desired length. Fasten off by making a backstitch or two, and remove the needle. Distribute the gathers evenly along the length of fabric.

**By Machine:** Set the machine for a long, wide, zigzag stitch, and knot one end of a long strand of heavy quilting thread or pearl cotton embroidery thread. Stitch over this thread, taking care not to stitch through the thread except perhaps at the knotted end. Pull the opposite thread end and slide the fabric toward the knot. When the gathered fabric is reduced to the required or desired length, wrap the free thread end around a pin to secure the gathers. Distribute the gathers evenly along the length of fabric.

## QUILTING

Quilting is a process of joining three layers together: a top, usually decorative, layer and a bottom/backing layer with batting in the middle.

Today's sewing machines have features that allow you to quilt projects very quickly and efficiently. Machine stitching is especially effective on overall gridline patterns or straight lines. But a number of people prefer to quilt by hand.

In some cases, such as kitchen linens, you'll discover that the tension on the vintage fabrics is different from the tension on yardage that you might purchase for a backing. The older fabrics seem to have been more tightly woven, and years of wear and laundering may have left them asymmetrical. If quilting by machine, feed fabrics through slowly, adjusting the tension and decreasing the pressure as necessary.

To guard against shifting between the top and backing, begin any quilting project by basting the layers securely together before you quilt. To baste the layers together, work from the top, starting at the center and working outward toward the edges vertically and horizontally, and then fill with diagonal lines in between. Pin the layers together around the edges before you start the basting stitches. The basting stitches will be cut and removed later as they are replaced with permanent quilt stitches.

There are several options as to where to place quilting stitches. You can choose to "outline-quilt," stitching around design patterns in the fabric such as flowers and borders. You can quilt in straight lines along seams, placing quilting stitches $1/4$ inch (6mm) from the seams. Or you can create a decorative quilting pattern, such as the heart-shaped one used on the Handkerchief Tablecloth/Quilt.

### Hand Quilting

For basting, use a sewing thread in a color that contrasts with the fabric so that it's easy to see when you remove it. Use heavyweight sewing thread or quilting thread for the permanent quilt stitching: In most cases, you will want to use white or a color that matches the fabric. If you are quilting a decorative design, choose a contrasting thread that will show off the stitches. Use a small (#8 or #9) sharp needle. Work with a strand of thread 15 to 18 inches (38 to 46cm) long. A frame or hoop is optional but preferable for best results.

To quilt, always begin from the center of the piece and work outward, stitching toward you. Turn the piece as you progress, so you can work outward in all directions evenly. To begin, thread the needle and knot one end. Insert the needle from the top 1 or 2 inches (2.5 or 5cm) from where you wish to begin stitching, guiding it through the batting only and bringing it out at the beginning of a stitching line. Give the thread a little tug to pull the knot through the quilt top and leave it buried in the batting. Make running stitches through all layers. Most quilters prefer to use thimbles to push the needle through. Keep the index or third finger of your nonstitching hand underneath your work to feel

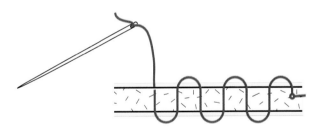

**Hand Quilting**

the needle's point and to make sure it penetrates all layers. Make one stitch at a time or load several onto the needle before pulling the thread all the way through. It's not as important to make tiny stitches as it is to strive for even, consistent-looking stitches. When you reach the end of the thread or the end of a stitching line, end off: Make a tiny backstitch and reinsert the needle at the same place, bringing it through the batting only and then out on top, a few inches away. Clip the thread close to where it emerges.

### Machine Quilting

Use sewing thread and a straight stitch, 6 to 8 stitches per inch (2 to 4 stitches per cm). Roll up the quilt or project to gain access to center areas, and work from the center outward.

# Pillow-making How-To's

Pillows can be made in a variety of shapes and sizes. The most popular style is a knife-edge pillow, the category into which the majority of pillows shown in this book fall even though they may have different edgings or backs. A box-edge pillow is practical if you want to display something on a flat surface. Fill your pillow covers with pillow forms, polyester fiberfill, or, in the case of shams, with standard bed pillows.

It's helpful when making a pillow to make a pattern even when you might mark directly on the fabric. To make a pattern, measure and mark the shape on tracing paper. Use a quilter's ruler or T-square to obtain straight lines and true, right corners for squares or rectangles, a compass to obtain a perfect circle or neat curves for the left and right top of a heart shape. If working with patterned fabric for the pillow top, draw your pattern on tracing paper (or other translucent paper) so that you will be able to see through the paper when positioning the pattern on the fabric to arrange designs to best advantage.

**Knife-Edge Pillow**

A knife-edge pillow is thicker at the center and tapers off at the edges. It consists of a same-size front, called the pillow top, and a same-size back. There may be trimming encased in the seam between the pillow top and back. When assembling the pillow cover, the top and back are stitched right sides together with one side left open to turn the cover right side out. This opening is then stitched closed by hand with slipstitches or with a zipper. You can make a closed (one-piece) back or an open overlapped back, which separates in the middle to allow you to insert a pillow form.

If fabric is heavy or apt to unravel or break apart, such as chenille or quilted fabrics, add ¹/₂ inch (13mm) for seam

allowances all around; otherwise, add only ¹/₄ inch (6mm) before cutting out the pillow top. If you wish your pillow to have a ruffle or piping, prepare the necessary amount following the directions on page 140-41 and apply it at this time.

**Stitching a Closed-Back Pillow**

**For a closed-back pillow**, cut a back the same size as the front. Pin pillow top on pillow back with right sides facing and edges even. Machine-stitch, using seam allowance as directed. (In the case of pillows trimmed with a sewn ruffle, piping (see page 140), fringe, etc., use a zipper foot to stitch slightly to the inside of previous basting.) Sew around 3 sides and corners of the fourth side. Cut across seam allowances at the corners. Turn pillow cover to the right side. Insert a pillow form, or, for nonstandard shapes such as hearts, stuff plumply with fiberfill. Turn the open edges to the inside and slipstitch the fourth side of the pillow closed.

**For an overlapped back**, cut 2 rectangles the same length as pillow top but 4 inches (10cm) shorter in width. For example, if your pillow top is 12 x 12 inches (30.5 x 30.5cm), you

will need to cut 2 squares that are 12 x 8 inches (20.5 x 30.5cm). (Length, always refers to the vertical measurement even if you are working with a square.) Overlap the rectangles until the outside edges match the width of the pillow top. Turn each of the overlapping edges ¼ inch (6mm) to wrong side and stitch, then turn another 2 inches (5cm) to wrong side and press from the back. Rearrange rectangles to overlap as before, so as to match pillow top dimensions. Pin and baste to secure. Pin pillow top on overlapping back sections, with right sides facing and outside edges even. Sew all around, leaving seam allowance as designated.

Clip across the seam allowances at the corners, and turn the pillow cover to the right side. Press. Insert the pillow form or bed pillow through the opening in the back. If desired, add small snaps, hooks, or hook-and-loop tape to close.

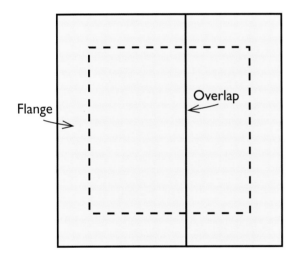

**An Overlapped Back with a Flange**

A flange, or tailored hem, such as that used on the Pretty Pastels Pillows, is a flat border along the edge of a knife-edge pillow cover. First, cut pillow top and back pieces equal to the pillow form plus the desired flange and seam allowances on four sides. After the pillow top and back are stitched together, turn the cover to the right side and, with a ruler or yardstick, mark and/or pin a line the allocated distance from the edge on all sides (ours are 2 and 2½ inches [5 and 6.5cm]). Topstitch along this line. Insert the pillow.

**Box Pillow**

A box-edge pillow consists of a pillow top and back plus a gusset or side panel, called the boxing strip, in between the pillow top and back. It's assembled in the same way as a knife-edge pillow with a closed back. If piping is required,

prepare the necessary amount according to the trimming how-to's on page 140 before constructing the pillow. There are square, rectangular, and round shapes, small and large—the settee cushion on page 33 is actually an oversize box pillow.

**For square or rectangular box pillows**, determine how deep you wish your box pillow to be; pillows shown throughout this book are approximately 2 to 4 inches (5 to 10cm) deep. Cut the boxing strip or strips 1 inch (2.5cm) wider for seam allowances. To determine the length of the boxing strips, measure the pillow top along each edge. Cut strips to these dimensions along the grain of fabric, usually the same fabric as pillow top and back.

For all stitching, pin pieces together with right sides facing and edges even. Stitch, leaving ½-inch (13mm) seam allowances throughout (unless otherwise indicated). First, stitch short edges of all the boxing strips together to make a ring. Press seams toward one side, as this will make them stronger. Apply piping to pillow top and/or back, if desired. Pin one long edge of boxing strip ring to pillow top, with right sides facing, edges even. Match corresponding edges and place seams at corners when possible; stitch. Pin and stitch pillow back to opposite long edge of ring in same manner, but leave an opening for turning. Clip into seam allowances at corners and along curves, as applicable. Turn cushion cover to right side. Insert a box cushion, or use a soft, slightly larger knife-edge pillow form and stuff corners with fiberfill if necessary. Turn open edges to inside and slipstitch closed.

**For a round box pillow**, follow individual directions for the project to cut 2 identical round circles for pillow top and back. Measure the circumference of the circle, and cut 1 boxing strip 1 inch (2.5cm) longer, and to a width that will produce the desired thickness of the pillow, plus seam allowances. Follow the directions for the square or rectangular box pillow to assemble the round box pillow, but ignore references to corners.

# Trimming How-To's

There are some projects, especially pillows and comforters, that you may decide to finish with a decorative edging. Piping (also referred to as cording or welting) and ruffles are the most popular choices. Piping can be used to accent the shape of a project or to provide a contrast color, as with some of the red piping on the Have-a-Heart Pillows. Ruffles not only add a feminine touch but also make the project larger. Double ruffles, two layers, are used on the doily pillows. Make (or purchase) your edging and sew it to the pillow or project top before attaching the backing.

### How To Make Piping

Piping in many colors is available in fabric stores. But if you'd like to use self-fabric, that is, the same fabric used for the pillow or quilt, or another fabric of your choice, make it yourself. To do so, measure or determine the circumference of the item to be piped and purchase cotton cording 2 inches longer, in standard $^1/_4$-inch (6mm) diameter or fatter widths. For example, a pillow that is 12 inches (30.5cm) square will have a circumferences of 48 inches (122cm), therefore, you will need to purchase 50 inches (127cm) of cording. Then you will need strips of fabric that will cover this cord, plus seam allowances. Use a tape measure to determine

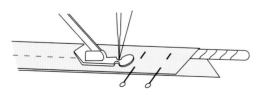

**Covering the Cord**

circumference of cord—$^1/_2$ inch (13mm) for standard $^1/_4$-inch (6mm) piping—and add two $^3/_8$-inch (1cm) seam allowances. Therefore, for standard piping, the width will be 1$^1/_4$ inches (3.5cm). Using a pencil or dressmaker's marking pencil, mark strips along the bias, that is to say, angled, rather than along the grain of the fabric. Piece the strips until they total the length of the cotton cording. Lay the cotton cording lengthwise down the center of the pieced fabric strip on the wrong side. Bring the long edges together. Using a zipper foot and thread to match fabric, machine-stitch close to the cotton cording.

### How to Apply Piping

To apply piping, pin it around pillow (or project) top, with right sides facing and raw edges even. Overlap piping ends by 1 inch (2.5cm). Cut open one end of piping and remove 1 inch (2.5cm) of cotton cording from inside. Fold under $^1/_4$ inch (6mm) of cut edge, then position this section over opposite end of piping; pin to secure. Baste piping in place as follows: Using a zipper foot and a long stitch length, machine-stitch as close to the cording as possible—slightly to the inside of the previous stitching line for piping. In this manner, sew all around, through all layers.

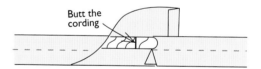

**Overlapping Piping Ends**

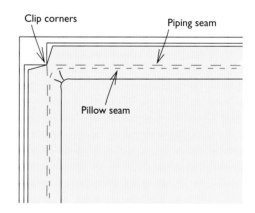

**Applying Piping**

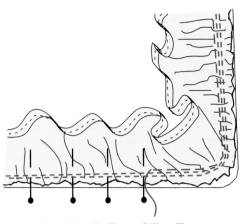

**Applying Ruffle to Pillow Top**

## How To Make a Ruffle

Cut strips of fabric as indicated for specific project, sewing multiple strips end to end in order to obtain the required total length. For a nice, full ruffle from medium-weight fabric, strive for twice the distance to be trimmed. For lightweight fabric, three times the distance will look very lush.

For a ruffle that will go all around an item, such as a pillow or coverlet, fold the strip crosswise in half, right sides facing, and pin the ends together. Stitch along the ends. Now you should have a large ring of fabric.

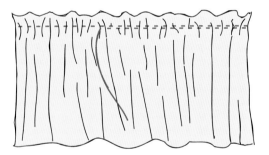

**Gathering Fabric For Ruffle**

**A hemmed ruffle** is a single layer of fabric finished at the outer edge it looks best from the front. To create it, hem one long edge by turning ¼ inch (6mm) to wrong side twice and stitching by machine; press.

**A folded ruffle** is a double layer of fabric, attractive from both sides. Avoid heavy fabric, as you will be stitching through many layers of fabric when it comes time to assemble the gathered piece together with the front and back. For this type of ruffle, fold the strip lengthwise in half, with wrong sides inside, and press.

In either case, gather the raw edges of the strip to the measurement of the circumference.

To pleat the fabric by folding it in even increments, see Step 3 of the Kitchen Linens Pillow on page 109.

## How To Apply Ruffles

Pin the ring around the pillow or quilt top, with right sides facing (folded ruffle has no wrong side) and raw edges even. Allow for more generous gathering or pleating at the corners of a project, so the ruffle fans out gracefully, and take care to hide ruffle seams within the gathers. Hand- or machine-baste the pieces together, a little less than a seam-allowance–width from the raw edges. When the project is assembled, these stitches will be concealed within the seam allowance.

## How To Apply Moss Fringe, Ball Fringe, and Other Trims

Pin trim around right side of pillow or quilt top, with straight edge of trim even with raw edge of pillow top. Stitch along the trim, a little less than a seam allowance–width from the edges, through both layers (trim and pillow or quilt top). For ball fringe, use a zipper foot attachment to machine-baste in place, close to inside edges of ball-fringe tape.

# Bibliography

*Cleary, David B. *Great American Brands: The Success Formulas That Made Them Famous.* New York: Fairchild Books, 1981.

Cook, Anna Lue. *Identification & Value Guide to Textile Bags (The Feeding & Clothing Of America).* Alabama: Books Americana, Inc., 1990.

*Cognac, Camille Dalphond. *Quilt Restoration: A Practical Guide.* Virginia: EPM Publications, 1994.

*Dolan, Maryanne. *Old Linens & Lace Including Crochet: An Identification & Value Guide.* Alabama: Books Americana, Inc., 1989.

Douglas, Maria Neder. *A Handmade Life: Ida Whaley Chance of Dalton.* Georgia: Agee Publishers, Inc., 1988.

*Gardner, Patricia L. *Handkerchief Quilts.* Virginia: EPM Publications, 1993.

*Jackson, F. Nevill. *Old Handmade Lace: With a Dictionary of Lace.* 1900. Reprint, New York: Dover Publications, 1987.

*Jorgensen, Janice. *Encyclopedia of Consumer Brands, Vol. II: Personal Products.* Washington, D.C.: St. James Press, 1994.

Johnson, Frances. *Collecting Antique Linens Lace & Needlework.* Pennsylvania: Wallace-Homestead Book Company, 1991.

*Johnson, Frances. *Collecting Household Linens.* Pennsylvania: Schiffer Publishing, Ltd., 1997.

Laury, Jean Ray. *New Uses for Old Laces.* New York: Doubleday & Company Inc., 1974.

*Orlofsky, Patsy and Myron Orlofsky. *Quilts in America.* New York: Abbeville Press, 1992.

*Palliser, Bury. *History of Lace.* Revised by J. Jourdain. New York: Dover Publications, 1984.

*Scofield, Elizabeth and Peggy Zlamea. *20th Century Linens & Lace.* Pennsylvania: Schiffer Publishing Ltd., 1995.

Stamper, Anita. *Treasured Trims: Mississippi Lace.* Hattiesburg: University of Southern Mississippi, 1984.

*The Lady's Pocket Companion and Indispensible Friend.* New York: Leavitt & Allen, circa 1840.

*A Hand-book of Etiquette for Ladies.* Philadelphia: George S. Appleton, Publisher, 1849.

* currently in print

## Periodicals and Pattern Books

*The Delineator, A Journal of Fashion, Culture and Fine Arts* (August 1894).

*McCall's Magazine* (December 1912 and January 1918).

*Home Needlework, A Magazine for Capable Women* (September 1916).

*Needlecraft Magazine* (October 1924, October 1928, and April 1929).

*Mother's-Home Life, and The Household Guest* (September 1938).

*The Workbasket* (March 1956, September 1957, December 1961, September 1962, February 1963, and June 1963).

*Conasauga, North Georgia's Magazine,* WW Communications, Inc. Dalton, Georgia.

*The Quarterly, Whitfield-Murray Historical Society,* Spring 1996, Dalton, Georgia (Spring 1996).

*Yankee,* July 1996, Yankee Publishing, Dublin, NH.

*Handkerchief Edgings,* Star Edging Book No. 102. New York: The American Thread Company, 1953.

*Crochet Treasures,* Star Treasure Book No. 126. New York: The American Thread Company.

*Laces and Edgings,* Book No. 199, Third Edition. The Spool Cotton Company, 1943.

*Flower Doilies and a New Pansy Doily,* Star Book No. 64. New York: The American Thread Company, 1949.

# Acknowledgments

I wish to express my appreciation to the many talented people who worked with me to produce and design the projects shown in this book.

## Embroidered Linens, Chapter One

Pillowcase Dolls, Dresser Scarf, and Teddy Bear, Betty DeVasto. All others, Rosemary Drysdale.

## Chenille, Chapter Two

Toddler's Jacket, Dolores Reiman; Throw Pillow with Green Ball-fringe, Nancy Lockwood. All others, Robin Tarnoff.

## Quilts, Chapter Three

Mounted Quilt Blocks, Annabelle Keller; Rag Doll and Duffel Bags, Barbara Ann Corniea; Pillows from Quilts, Laura Fisher and Jean Wilkinson; Door Knob Hanger, Theo Taylor; Patchwork Teddy Bear and Window Shade and Balloon Valance, Robin Tarnoff; Place Mats, Pamela J. Hastings; Angel Ornament, Mary Fallone; Patchwork Rabbit, Jean Wilkinson.

## Lace Trims, Chapter Four

Long-Stem Roses, Betty DeVasto; Lace Angel, Kathleen George; Victorian-House Wall Hanging, Shirley Botsford; Shelf Edging, Dressed-up T-Shirts and Lace-Trimmed Lamp Shades, Rosemary Drysdale; Patches-of-Lace Pillow and Woven-Lace Pillow, Barbara Ann Corniea.

## Handkerchiefs, Chapter Five

Floral-Print Handkerchief Wreath, Kathleen George; Tablecloth/Quilt, Michele Crawford; Holiday Handkerchief Angel, Betty DeVasto; Merry Christmas Wall Hanging, Pat Long Gardner; Three Little Kitten Dolls, Robin Tarnoff; Christmas Stockings, Have-a-Heart Pillows, and Sachets, Rosemary Drysdale.

## Kitchen Linens, Chapter Six

Annabelle's Sundress, Dolores Reiman; Tablecloth Teddy, Christmas Cloth Tote, and Christmas Stockings, Robin Tarnoff; Fruit-and-Floral Kitchen Set, Strawberry Coverlet and Pillow Sham, Grapevine Wreath, and Ruffled Floor Pillows, Rosemary Drysdale.

## Doilies, Chapter Seven

Wreath Ornaments, Kathleen George; Doily Collage, Jeannie Oberholtzer. All others, Rosemary Drysdale.

With heartfelt gratitude to Vivian Aufhauser, Cathy Cook, Laura Fisher, Shari E. Hartford, Penny Dunlap Ladnier, Francis X. Morrissey, Jr., Jean Wilkinson, Marcelle White, and to everyone on the IFDA Membership Committee who shared their time, their friendship, and their expertise to make this book possible.

Special thanks to the following corporations and their representatives, who provided products and information and were always available as project consultants, especially Sharon Currier for Styrofoam, Jane Schenck for Pellon, Donna Wilder for Fairfield, and Ellie Schneider for Offray.

STYROFOAM® Brand Products
The Dow Chemical Company
1610 Building
Midland, MI 48674-0001

All fusibles: Wonder-Under®, Heavy-Duty Wonder Under®, Wonder-Web®, Wonder-Shade®, and Pellon® Fusible Fleece by Pellon®
Freudenberg Nonwovens
3440 Industrial Drive
Durham, NC 27704

Polyester pillow forms, Pop-In-Pillow®, Low-Loft®, Ultra-Loft® and Hi-Loft® bonded polyester battings by Fairfield Processing Corporation
88 Rose Hill Avenue
P.O. Box 1130
Danbury, CT 06813-1130

All ribbons by
C.M. Offray & Son, Inc.
Route 24, Box 601
Chester, NJ 07930

Fabric stiffener, Stiffy®, by
Plaid Enterprises Inc.
Norcross, GA 30091

All self-adhesive hook-and-loop fasteners by
Velcro® USA Inc.
6420 East Broadway Blvd.
Tuscon, AZ 85710